SLEEPING
with
THE DOGS

Chad Ehlers

Library of Congress Control Number: 2021919183
ISBN-13: Paperback: 978-1-64749-613-5
        ePub: 978-1-64749-614-2

Printed in the United States of America

GoToPublish LLC
1-888-337-1724
www.gotopublish.com
info@gotopublish.com

The dog house I live in is a million dollar four bedroom, three bath family home with a seldom used swimming pool in back and the number 4 painted on the curb in front. It is the only thing that distinguishes our house from all the other equally clean brown houses that line both sides of these endless cul de sacs in another bedroom community, this one called Laguna Niguel in sunny Southern California.

I didn't always sleep with dogs, in fact I once slept with most any woman that would allow me, the only criteria being that it was definitely a woman and that she was good looking. . . . which of course can be subjective. Sleeping with women around the world may have a lot to do with why I now sleep with three dogs instead of my beautiful, much younger and sexier wife who sleeps in the same house, only one floor up with our fourth dog. How this came about is part of a long twisted tale, a personal journey and one I have avoided putting on paper for at least 15 years. The stories that follow are small visual pieces of a huge personal puzzle that will never be complete, recollections from this one person's life, the kind of tales usually shared between bar stools or at some dinner table with anyone willing to listen. It is a collection of memories, bits of history that need to be put on paper soon, now, or remain forever unwritten. . . and part of a very short bucket list.

What does eventually find its way into these memoirs is all true. Nothing fictitious or fabricated. . . which is one of the reasons I now sleep with the dogs. I am brutally honest, to the point it usually causes arguments with both my wife and my 13 year old daughter. I am not good at swallowing thoughts, my version of right. I love honesty even when it hurts, especially when it hurts. I never know when to keep my version of the truth to myself, to keep my big mouth shut. My golf buddies have tried to warn me that in marriage there are only two choices. . . . to be right or to be happy. I live in this constant conflict between right and happy with a wife who has been going through menopause forever. . . and a daughter just starting puberty. It is a life between the rock and a hard place. Another reason I often stick with the dogs, the only members of our million dollar four bedroom mortgage free residence that listen to me without arguing, that continue to love me in spite of my faults, and who I can love back without swallowing

Cialis or Viagra pills. I love sex but hate drugs, and the testosterone levels are waning while my age keeps waxing!

How I ended up in this mess is the story, one that is probably similar to thousands, if not millions of others living in these sterile vanilla villages run by management companies, idiots that have the right to tell home owners what color to paint their own dwellings, choices limited to six different shades of brown. The journey to these cul de sacs may be different for everyone, but in the end the results are pretty much the same. Kids going to decent local schools, mortgages, two cars in the garage, a TV in every bedroom, home insurance, car insurance, health insurance, earthquake insurance, life insurance. . . and taxes, a myriad of taxes equal to the number of pages you signed with your realtor when you bought your bank owned palace. It's a rut, one you learn to enjoy while constantly complaining.

Somebody once told me the only difference between a rut and the grave is the depth.

Some of us need to start digging, but first we need to figure out which way is up. . . otherwise the rut only gets deeper. So here is a journey of words, a personal narrative that helps me dig while I try to figure out which way up is? This narrative also helps keep me out of the booze cabinet, a place my wife has been visiting with ever greater frequency while we share our sleigh ride through So Cal society/insanity!

I didn't get married until I was 53 and did not have my first and only child until I was 56. You might say I was not made for a life of routine and responsibility and luckily I became aware of that at a fairly young age. My older brother married his high school sweet heart and had a son 7 months later. Amazingly more than 50 years have passed, and they are still together the son still living in the back guest house. Responsibility was not the right road for me, the younger of two boys who grew up in Manhattan Beach, running along sandy shores and enjoying Granddad's pile of National Geographic magazines. The sounds of the shore and those magazine images sent me out another door, the one with 'adventure' written on it, the one that Jack Kerouac wrote about in "Life on the Road", minus the drugs. A road that carried me beyond the boundaries of the USA. That life of a highway hobo is one I shall return to later, but for now I want to get back to the present, to the wife, dogs, daughter and sedation. For now parenthood, and later to the road that lead me back to So Cal and this sterilization.

It started long before I took that happy hike down a Catholic Church aisle in Buenos Aires. Before signing away my freedom south of the border a lot of fun loving romantic water had gone under the bridge. Waters that were teaming with female fish and seven warm years in Hawaii taught me a little about fishing. The social sport of catch and release started in the islands. Wedding bells at the age of 53 means you are bringing more than the average amount of mental baggage (fish stories) with you to the reception. Hell, even while waiting for my wife to arrive at the church that night (a hour late) I was still gazing at a fine collection of beautiful Argentine females that filled the brides side of the aisle. So was the priest I might add. He even suggested I stroll down the aisle, get a feeling for it and take a closer look those female friends of the bride just in case my first choice for the night didn't show up. He reminded me that the service was already paid for. Nothing like a priest who enjoys a good drink and bit of humor... and speaks two languages. (On my side of the aisle there was one body, sleeping, an old inebriated gentleman who had come in out the rain snoozing in back pew.) Anyway, what I am trying to say is that I had already recorded a diary full of exotic and erotic dates, the by-products of which were destined to turn me into a fairly jaded husband. Luckily I was going down this first church aisle with a lovely tall Korean lady, one whose first language was Spanish. She was marring a man who could not speak a word of Spanish, and had been on this planet 17 years longer. A man that would now need to go from his catch and release addictions to fidelity. Or maybe just another guy who had no clue what routine sex would feel like 16 years into a marriage? Does anyone? Does anyone care in the beginning? Luckily everyone thinks it's not the destination, but the journey that counts. With marriage it should be the other way around?

Proudly I remained faithful all those years in spite of my wife's doubts, addictions and accusations. But in retrospect I wonder if it was actually wise to have put away all my fishing gear? I reckoned after years of trolling in Hawaii and around the globe, that one more fish was not going to make much difference. Was I just getting too old, leaking testosterone? Being with a lovely younger woman does help keep you pacified and focused! She was supposed to be my last fish. But then a life of love with one woman is challenging after a life of lust with many. It's part of the reason I am now sleeping with the dogs. Spoiled, under motivated, short on lust, or testosterone. . . and long on memories! What about those memories?

When I think back it is usually the person that makes the place, sometimes vice versa? For sure the craziest places and finest bodies linger the longest.

It was a lifestyle many old timers have in common, meeting ladies face to face instead via on-line dating services or computerized connections, places where you could actually see what you were getting like on the street, in a market or restaurant or best of all, on a nice sunny beach. . . in a tiny bikini before the days of silicone. Ask any guy who grew up in the 60's and 70', a period some call the 'pre-aids era'. Sex was fun, accepted, routine and fairly safe. By today's standard very safe! Any healthy body and spirit who was single thirty, forty or fifty years ago would have similar amorous tales to tell, at least those who did not get married right out of high school or college. Those residing in convents and monasteries were teaching sex education. Drugs, sex and music were the common hat trick. I passed on the drugs and then doubled down on the other two. Never even smoked a cigarette, and to this day still haven't. Just got high on music, nature and bodies. . . all of which were everywhere and all of which you couldn't get enough of. It was not complicated. All you needed was enough money to pay the rent, food, gas, beer and wine. Music, nature and women were never in short supply and were established members of the new Hawaiian culture.

On to some of those faces and places that helped spoil a healthy road runner, and a perfectly normal marriage. This is a pretty common story, people having physical fun, of trying to dutifully enjoy every day and every person to the fullest potential without feeling shame or neurosis. The science of hormone behavior. All of us were experimental rats.

Our past is a palette of colorful memories, colors used to paint mental images for others. My personal palette is mostly a travelogue, one that blends scenic places with sensory moments such as:

The shores of Hawaii, especially the north shore of Oahu. Not Banzai Pipeline, Sunset, or Waimea Bay but quieter shores between Kahaluu and Laie and even out toward Makaha. I lived and made love all over Oahu during my seven years in Hawaii, especially when I lived in Kahala and Waikiki, (walked naked on Kuhio Avenue after work at 3 am with Cindy), shared an old marlin fishing boat mounted with eight speakers, two guys and three naked ladies on the Kona Coast (leaving Keauhou boat harbor every morning to the sounds of the Steve Miller Band, The Moody Blues and Crosby, Stills, Nash and Young with sun rising behind silhouetted Mouna Loa and Kilauea), rolling with naked ladies on the beaches of Anahola and Hanakapiai on Kauai and then a short time in Lahaina, Maui. I spent the best seven years of my life in Hawaii in the late 60's and early 70's, much of it in an apt. one block behind the Market Place in Waikiki where I was helping manage five of Honolulu's finest, long forgotten, restaurant/night clubs. Even the wooden statue in one of our restaurants got laid. Anyone above ground was getting the leg over. Every bar tender, waiter, manager, car park, bus boy or active member of the tourist business was smiling. The taxi and bus drivers bringing in all those anxious new faces from Honolulu Airport were the lead off batters. The turnover for most of us was weekly, daily, and sometimes even hourly.

Your job, your gift of gab and your looks did count, but everyone with a pulse was enjoying the party. I spent five years on bikini patrol along the shores of Waikiki, some of it while in the Coast Guard, and all of it causing serious eye strain. Sex was the drug of choice for most and there was plenty to go around. Waves of women just kept rolling onto the Hawaiian shores from all parts of the planet. Each one seeking a week or two of fun in the sun, far from their 9-5 routines and responsibilities back home. For all of us, tourists, locals and kamaainas, every day counted. Sometimes ladies you met soon after arriving would come knock on your door on their way back to the airport for one last hour of Aloha (a word that also means love and affection). For seven hard years (not literally) I did my part, fulfilling any and all entertainment responsibilities. After seven years of this frivolous fun, something new did seem necessary, something that could stimulate the other brain, elevate my principles, rewards wrapped in different scenery and clothing, cerebral as well as carnal. It was time to try and visit some of those places the lovely ladies vacationing in Hawaii were coming from. I had no idea then that this need to explore would take half a lifetime. It turned out to be the better half, at least artistically and morally. The challenge soon became how to discover romantic moments unaided by offshore sea breezes, leaning palm trees, bikinis, and Hawaiian music blended with bodies, waves and sunshine?

Eventually this gift of gab found its voice in new places... such as:

Amsterdam, my first stop in Europe, (leaving my backpack with a Dutch student I met while watching the 1970 World Cup in a pub, then hitching rides out to such towns and cities as Alkmaar, Breda, Enschede, Utrecht and Zandvoort). Then the liberated city of Copenhagen where I lived for nearly a year with a Danish lady between delivering rent-a-cars all over Europe, (a city filled with Scandinavia beauties, including one particular hooker that had more stories to share than Johnny Carson or Uncle Remus, then Paris (which included a lovely rare red head working at EuroDisney in the ticket booth, try that with a line of 20 behind you waiting), then London (mostly, but not only with my Irish girlfriend of 10 years who also teamed with me and her mother in Ireland for a ride around the Dingle Peninsula on the County Kerry by horse and cart), the Lofoten Islands (in Northern Norway) and Vardo also in Northern Norway where I worked on a cod fishing boat one summer and luckily met the local baker's daughter. Even on our way up the Norwegian coast on a fishing boat, meeting some lady working in a photo shop in Hammerfest that later won the football lotto (and spent her winnings taking me to Costa Del Sol, Spain for two weeks), then Helsinki (with a tango champion and then a very delicate Finnish butterfly in the fields and forests across Finland (even while cross country skiing), then my favorite city Prague (a place I visited 22 times during the cold war. . . . in which I was never cold), Gdansk, Poland (with a girl I met at the Louvre in Paris), Stockholm, Stockholm, Stockholm (I could fill pages with lovely memories from Stockholm and every other part of Sweden during 25 years, 14 of which were spent lecturing in 100 different high schools or gymnasiums. Luckily the legal age was 16 and graduating age 19), San Sebastian (with a girl I met in Cordoba, Argentina), in fields near Toledo and later Madrid, then Venice (in that tiny beach hut), and Salamanca, Spain (in mountain streams naked with a beauty from Germany), Freiburg in the Black Forest (by some German lady that ran me off the autobahn at nearly 80 mph just to share wine at a rest stop and then later at her home), in Bahia, Brazil (a petite Brazilian in a shower I still think about), in Buenos Aires (where I eventually met my wife while staying with another lovely Argentine woman that later visited me in Laguna Beach, California, including getting naked on a warm sand dune in Death Valley). Argentina eventually ended a great run. (Perhaps it was payback, otherwise known as marriage. . . . or purgatory), Cordoba (two different ladies hours apart at the same hotel and same cafe served by the same waiter with his shit eating grin. . . . Cordoba what a place to meet the ladies!!), Caracas and then again on Margarita Island with the same beautiful Venezuelan blond(that nearly lost her life in a rain forest on St. Lucia Island in the Caribbean. We found out the hard way why they are called 'rain forests'! Not funny), then the Cook Islands (Aitutaki), French Polynesia (Huahine and Moorea), Sydney, I think I struck out in Auckland, Tokyo (where they tend to giggle a lot, before, during and after), Seoul (but that was with my wife which doesn't count), Bangkok (the Hawaii of the Far East. . . in Thailand you usually have to pay to play. Lucky Luke got lucky with a bar owner who didn't need the money and owned a big house). The Maldives, an extremely romantic place as was the Seychelles, Paris again (meeting the wildest woman of all, an American who professed to be the world's best and then tried to prove it in a petite Paris hotel). I could not wait to see her again and it happened in California at my Dad's place in San Juan Capistrano. Dad was not happy, Chad was. (Scary but fun!)

How many times did we use Dad's place in Manhattan Beach where we grew up? How many close calls jumping off balconies or through windows to escape getting caught by parents, yours or hers, creating exits where there were none previously.

The escapes often were more exciting than the sex. Laguna Beach where I lived above Woods Cove on and off for 10 years. So many wonderful places, faces and memories from different parts of the states. . . besides Hawaii. Fort Lauderdale (with Linda whom I met while working as a bag boy for some market and then flown to the Bahamas in her ex-husband's plane. Weird. As I said, the strange memories do last). New York City (with a lovely Puerto Rican girl met previously in Hawaii), Boston (another girl met in Hawaii), New Orleans at the Mardi Gras (with a fellow tourist from the Big Apple in her hotel on Bourbon Street from which the manager tossed me. We continued that perfect night weeks later in NYC at her place), then the beautiful black woman met at the airport when leaving New Orleans for NYC whose boyfriend played for the Jets (happily surviving an early exit the next morning), down in Mississippi and the Gulf Coast and throughout New England with a Swedish girl that went on to make millions as the Pantene girl in Pantene and Oil of Olay hair commercials, then during a ride across the states on a Greyhound Bus with a fellow passenger who came aboard in the middle of the night in Kansas (the big black lady across the aisle giving me and my bouncing lap blanket the evil eye,). No one ever got hurt. . . or even pregnant. . . luckily! Some of it was pure foolishness and all of it harmless fun. It seemed like a great way to grow up. On the loose, road running with the Nikon kids (camera). Writing it down now is just a way of trying to preserve or share a few of those special moments, a way of xeroxing the past, if only for myself? It is a dilemma common to others who have great stories and memories to share.

Why do it? It's your own blood leaking out onto paper. Perhaps just for family, but should my daughter even be allowed to read this? Oh well, let it ride now and see what happens later.

I will return to some of these aforementioned romantic places and faces later. A few are worthy of a little embellishment. In fact before weaving my way back to the beginning let me record that very first time, the first naked lady. That is an odd moment few of us forget. For me it happened in the least romantic place I have ever lived, Arcata, California, Humblodt County, my second year of college at Humboldt State. Yes, still a virgin going into that sophomore year, still interested more in sports than Playboy Magazine or sex. I was living in some dumpy trailer below campus with a tall weird flamenco guitar player who was not a virgin. A pretty lady (rare in those parts) had been coming around the trailer trying to coax me into bed, trying to steal my virginity, and I wanted to pass her off to my roommate who was the horny member of our aluminum abode and old enough to buy booze legally. That particular night she came, he bought, I left, she drank, he didn't score, she didn't leave, I return, she's intoxicated, I'm nervous, she's not, she undresses, I stare, she crawls into bed, I don't crawl out, she's upstairs, I'm downstairs, she turns into the energizer bunny, I'm frozen, she lets go, not of me, I let fly, she's happy, I'm confused?

The next morning my roommate wants to celebrate my lost virginity with some fellow trailer rats but I tell him to hold off on the invitations. I try to explain the jury is still out. He's not having it. You did or you didn't. I choose option three. . . maybe! I was somewhere warm and wet, but I know not where? Only one thing was sure. . . . . I needed to try that again.

Round one left me equally aroused and confused? Were men meant to be on the bottom? Dustin Hoffman in the Graduate was far ahead of me. At least I had located the starting blocks, not how to finish the race? So next semester I am back in Southern California going to El Camino Junior College, the year that Kennedy got shot, and trying find someone to help me get back into the starting blocks. Linda Smiley.

I ran into an old grammar school girlfriend's sister working for Sears at the Torrance Mall and decided to drop by her house. I knew the family well having been chased for two years around the playgrounds by this girls younger sister who was as ugly and skinny as a duck gets, catching snakes that everyone else ran from, with freckles, braids and braces, braces that were put into her mouth by my orthodontist, the one we visited monthly together. I always sat on the opposite side of the waiting room from this whack job.

After leaving Torrance High and attending Temple City High for two years, then going off to college for two more, I was back four years later hoping for a date with the older sister. The house looked the same. What answered the door did not. Some playboy bunny, an erotic dream, the younger sister, that same skinny freckle-faced whack job that once chased me around our grammar school playground. Her name was Linda Smiley (the name is not changed to protect anyone, in fact I hope she might find this before we both are history). No longer the ugly duck with braids and braces, but a beautiful statuesque 20 year old, one very gorgeous young lady that still liked me... the perfect 10. The perfect starting gun! This lovely bird was already sporting titles of Miss Torrance, Miss El Camino College and runner up in some Miss Las Vegas contest. We quickly laugh our way out to my 56 Chevy, drove one whole block over to our grammar school parking lot and dove into the back seat. Rain was dancing on the roof as we eliminated raiment. She helped guide me into the normal top gunner position, not the one implanted on my brain at Humboldt State. Strangely junior got confused, panicked, could not get out of the starting blocks. The voluptuous body below lay naked on bright red naugahyde upholstery from Tijuana waiting patiently. No bang, no race!

My face was as red as the naugahyde? Linda asks "what's the deal with junior?" 'Nothing'. There was no such thing a Cialis back then, and at age 20 you had better not need it! Certainly not on top of this amazing torso!

The problem must have been her 36 natural double D anti-aircraft guns? HaHaHa. Something about being upstairs... but that was too embarrassing to discuss so we both buttoned up. Linda gives me a curious smile, (Linda Smiley) and I drive the whole block back to her place. Shit, junior works, the girl that night in the cheap trailer loudly confirmed that. Next night Linda and I try again, same grammar school parking lot, same back seat, same wet weather.... same result! Shit, now we are both feeling too embarrassed to talk. Something wrong with the starting blocks, well starting position. It's amazing how people can be fixated, even traumatized by previous events.

I knew nothing was wrong with that kid Linda once happily chased around only yards away from where we were now laying naked ... but how to prove it?

Strike two and waiting for that third pitch when I get the nerve to suggest a position change, putting my naked butt on the Mexican naugahyde.

Bingo. Smiley is all smiles. Weird beats worthless. Soon all parts were good to go. Eventually I did learn that being on top also works. So that was graduation night. Nearly 21.

As the old saying goes, better late than never!

SLEEPING WITH THE DOGS –
II - UNARMED SERVICE

Nothing like a three year break between pages when writing about yourself. One of the benefits of doing something for play rather than pay.

What happened to those three years? Poof, gone. Improved my golf handicap by one. The truth is my back went to the complaint department after only two days of concentrated (constipated) sitting in this office chair playing on this keyboard. It felt just like the first herniated disk I celebrated 20 years ago in Sweden the day after lifting some old snow tires out my car trunk and hauling them up to the attic. That lovely pain back then took a full year to get over. This time just the fear of another herniated disc caused me to take a three year sabbatical from writing. OK, spines have a right to complain, especially after registering some forty road running fun loving years with a backpack riding on it. Turns out that sitting can be even harder on those vertebrates than cranking a bike, hiking a mountain, swinging a golf club or wheeling a tennis racquet. If that proves true again, this labor of love will likely never get finished. I also sense another growing issue and serious challenge with this kind of writing. The past and the present don't grow closer together with each passing year. Memory doesn't improve with age as do some wines. One more cranky L-1 to L-5 vertebrae could force me into an early retreat with Uncle Jackie (JD - Jack Daniels) rather than with some computer keyboard.

Anyway, nothing much changed the past three years, all the dogs are still alive, likewise with my daughter and me, she jumped overnight from 13 to 16 and is finally a bit easier to deal with.... oh yes, I did get divorced. The older you get the less you try to invite pain into your life, especially emotional pain. Divorce was unavoidable. . . . and extremely distressing! I may get back to what that was all about some pages later, but for now its onward into the past.

There is becoming a greater sense of urgency with these memoirs.

The beginning.

Life for this Aries (April 18) began in Manhattan Beach, California. It doesn't get much better than Manhattan on this planet. . . a lovely sandy shore paints the western front of this sleepy beach town. Fishing off the pier, swimming in the Pacific, running barefoot along the beaches, playing marbles on white sands that actually covered parts of our grammar school playgrounds. Loved the game of marbles and had collected about 10,000 in a big wooden barrel by the time I was 12. They didn't impress my very first girlfriend, Michelle McCutcheon (where you are today?), so I gave them to some church. Mom raised my older brother and I on her own in a lovely cottage condo on 12th street, one of eight cottages my Grandparents owned and managed. . . . and then finally sold for 66 grand to buy a place down in Seal Beach Leisure World. Those same cottages on 12th street recently resold for north of 7 million. Bummer! Why weren't we all blessed back then with a little better foresight? So it goes!

Len, my brother, was three years my senior, still is, and as of today has been married to the same lady for over 54 years, his high school sweetheart from Torrance HS. The day after I was born my Dad did a hospital drive by, the proud sire of a second healthy boy, Kenny, to go with Lenny. The next two kids by his second wife were Terry and Sherry. (Not a lot of imagination. . . . or sense of responsibility). Years later at Dad's 50th wedding anniversary Len and I concluded that by the time Dad arrived at the hospital to see how many legs I had he was married to two women simultaneously, one being my Mom. Back then Dad did not hang around for long. Today such fathers are fondly known as Disneyland Dads, or in our case, literally "Good Time Charlie". His first name was Chuck. Two buck Chuck. Dad stopped being Good Time Charlie when he ran out of gas somewhere near the age of 80. Mom is now 99 and may never run out of gas. She lives in Sedona, Arizona, in a retirement center where she teaches ballroom dancing. She is still sporting her own teeth, her own eyes, ears and limbs, all of which still work perfectly. She has added a pig's valve to her heart, thus her nickname, "Little Miss Piggy". She has the bone density of a 40 year old. In fact she is so damn healthy that both my brother and I have put her in our living wills. After divorce there is not that much left for me to bequeath her.

Back to Manhattan and youth. There was some real upside to having Grandparents living next door. Warm hearts to share with as well as warm meals and a Granddad who loved to go camping and fishing, plus a Grandmother willing to go along. Every summer while Mom was working as a dental hygienist the Grandparents would round up the big tent, canvas tarps, Coleman stove and lantern, fishing poles, sleeping bags, necessary utensils and their two Grandchildren and pack them all into an old Nash Rambler, then set off up Highway 5 toward the small town of Yreka in the Shasta Valley near Mount Shasta. From there it was over to the sleepy little village of Fort Jones with its wooden boardwalks, and eventually down the Scott River to our lovely isolated summer home called the Springflats campground. Two hidden, unused fire pits are all that remain today. We were usually the first ones into Springflats every summer and the park rangers were on first name basis with Granddad. We would clean up the wooden outhouse nearest our campsite, nail up a couple wooden crates high on the trees so bears would have to at least stand on their hind legs to reach the bacon and beans, lay out the camping gear, get the rods and reels ready for action and pull out the cribbage board. My brother and Grandad caught most of the fish and Grams did most of the frying. Stray cats came in from all directions every summer to enjoy the left over scraps of trout. Finally we took one stray home with us, Spussy. She lived to be 19 and never once slept in the house in Manhattan. . . . but then she had 8 cottages to roam around and sleep under. I later did the same when I ran away from home after my Mother remarried and moved over to Torrance. I used to find Spussy under the main house when I went into hiding there. Moving so far inland was a downer. No more ocean, no more running barefoot from the Manhattan Pier to the Redondo Breakwater.

Back to Springflats. Years later we asked the Grandparents how they happened to pick such a remote faraway place to go camping and they said they took out a California road map, closed their eyes and stuck in a pin. The little hole in that California map turned out to be Springflats, a place that left us all with three summers of joyful impressions and memories, and helped shape the minds and habits of two young boys. You've heard of the famous 'Hole in the Wall Gang' from the American Wild West. Len and I were the 'Hole in the Map Boys'. Not quite as famous, but part of a West that was becoming less wild by the day. Our quartet would stay nearly three months every summer, the only outlet to civilization provided by our weekly drive in the Nash Rambler along a winding dirt road paralleling the Scott River into Fort Jones. Grandparents got ice and a slice of meat to put something on our menu besides trout. Len and I would head over to the old drug store for a new comic book, a soda and an ice cream cone. Life was simple. . . and good. I could fill a few pages with just those three summers, memories of snagging crayfish, dodging rattle snakes, facing off bears, watching Granddad chase them out of camp at night, naming cats, feeding cats, catching squirrels, picking berries, meeting campground neighbors, watching moths race around the Coleman lantern over a nightly game of cribbage, cicadas and river sounds rather than radio, television, computer or cell phones. The best jump start a kid could have.

I wish it had never ended. . . but the only permanence is change. The beach was now gone. Two years at Torrance High School followed by two years at Temple City High School. Mom and my stepfather kept getting further away from the Pacific Ocean. Torrance High just happened to be the school where Louis Zamperini went, the American hero and subject of the book and movie "Unbroken". He ran long distance and set the high school mile record of 4. 21. 2 clear back in 1934, a record us runners were still trying to break thirty years later. I managed to get within a couple of seconds of Zamperini's time while at Temple City which was good enough to snag me a track (athletic) scholarship to the University of Utah. So now off to college, and even further away from the Pacific . . . in fact a mile above the ocean. Good old Rocky Mountain high. . . actually too high for my lungs and legs.

The U of U did not turn out to be a perfect fit for this low altitude barefoot runner.

That athletic scholarship lasted a year. One and done.

The main fun in sports came not from running but from quarterbacking intramural football teams, first at the U of U, then San Jose State and eventually back to El Camino Community College in Torrance. While attending El Camino College John F. Kennedy was assassinated, on Nov. 22, 1963. I was in the activities center watching it on TV along with half the student body. It changed a lot of our lives. The army and Vietnam were now waiting for a lot of college students. My draft date was getting closer bringing with it likely opportunities for a military job in Southeast Asia. It was time for a lot of us to find a branch of the service that did not require getting drafted.... or shot at. It was also time to get acquainted with that lovely term serendipity "fortunate happenstance or pleasant surprise". Fortune and surprise became friends that served me well at a time I was supposed to be serving my country well. It started with being lucky enough to locate a benign version of military duty called the US Coast Guard Reserve. Have no fear, this is not the harsh tale of personal suffering. Quite the opposite and therefore I recommend that those who served our country in a war zone, or anything even close to combat, should just by-pass the next few pages I shall title...

"How to Enjoy the Military Without Really Trying"

Everything that follows happened pretty much as written without embellishment.

Writers are allowed some 'artistic license' but I promise to avoid over doses.

How to dodge the draft bullet? For me there was no escape. I did not hold any cards from the deferment deck, ie., student deferment, physical disability, conscientious objector, religious conflict, mental illness (questionable), well connected parent, rich parent, Swedish passport, Swedish girlfriend.... or desertion. About two weeks down the calendar was my D day (draft day), the day of my Army physical. Being named athlete of the year at Temple City HS, then winning the physical fitness competition at El Camino Community College and Long Beach State did not lend themselves to a resume for a physical deferment. I would not be failing the Army physical. The time to panic had already set in. If you were around back then you knew the feeling. Either you wanted to go where the bullets were flying, or you didn't. I didn't. Not even of fond hunting rifles, so I put a full tank of gas in my old Austin Healey Sprite and headed north, up the California coast in search of a place to hide in the form of a reserve unit; Air National Guard, Army Reserves, Naval Reserves or better yet Coast Guard Reserves.... the perfect fit for a naturalized beach boy. After heading north on Highway 101 and knocking on all the doors, it became apparent I was arriving about two years too late. Every military unit I visited just laughed and then asked if I'd like to put my name on their growing waiting list, lists as long as phone books. I continued my quest clear up to the Oregon border and then thought about continuing the journey right on into Canada, one sure but desperate way to escape the draft.

After contemplating that option, the Sprite made a U-turn and headed south. It seems I was years late for the "reserve" party. On the return drive there was one place I had bypassed on the way north due its size and popularity, the San Francisco Coast Guard Headquarters. If all the smaller units had two year waiting lists, prospects in the City by the Bay did not seem promising. What the hell. Finding parking was hard enough, finding a way out of the draft felt impossible? At least the San Francisco office had air conditioning along with more of those same white uniforms,one of which was about to get a chuckle at my expense. I asked the kid behind the front desk if they had a place in the reserves, the kicker being I had only two weeks before going in for my physical.

The guy did laugh, but then magically said, "Too bad you are not from Humboldt County. One of the two guys from up there had to cancel yesterday and we need to fill his spot." "But I am from Humboldt County, I live in Arcata" I said. You can find my name and address in the phone book. " (My brother actually lived in Arcata. Still does. Good enough... and I had attended Humboldt State College for one whole semester).

Are you able to go in tomorrow. . . and are you prepared to spend the duration of your military obligation living in Humboldt County?"

'You bet your sweet ass I am.'

And off to lunch this guy and I went, enjoying small talk over a bowl of chili and a Budweiser. "By the way" I asked, "What was that part about - 'spending the duration of my military obligation in Humboldt County? "Can the Coast Guard really do that?" He said come on back to the office and let me show you what it says in the military manual, a book about as thick as the Oxford English Dictionary. He plopped the manual on his desk, pried it open to a page, a section and finally a paragraph that read something like this,,, 'If deemed necessary due to unavoidable fiscal, monetary or academic responsibilities, the military will waiver your obligation to reside in the area originally assigned. . . . . etc,.' Well, something like that. It was my ticket out of Dodge (Humboldt), and he affirmed it with a wink and a hand shake. I would not likely have to spend 6 years in Humboldt County! Hallelujah! I found my car and started driving around San Francisco and then down to San Jose near one of the many state college that I had attended, just trying to nervously enjoy those last few hours before entering active duty.

Coast Guard boot camp -

A friend over in San Jose agreed to store my Austin Healey for a few months. I then found a ride to the Coast Guard Base at Alameda with some spoiled California kid in his giant Lincoln Continental. Can't recall how we met? I do recall that he ran that big Lincoln into some freeway off ramp guard rail and then just laughed it off. Actually we both laughed it off. The nervous energy was growing . . . and contagious. The anxiety continued to mount right on over to the base at Alameda Island and then on into those initial hours when 64 new Coast Guard recruits assemble for the first time in one big room. All males, kids in their late teens or early twenties, smiling, talking trash, sharing high fives, still sporting individual hair styles and clothing, tossing their testosterone around like it was some fraternity party. This would be a party enjoyed by few. The next day they took everyone over to the barber to get scalped, and then to some kind of locker room where all the private duds were collected. Next came our new boot camp rags and gear, our assigned new look. The days of personal style and choices and arrogance were over. For the first time everyone's individual clothing and looks were gone, kids with nothing familiar to talk about or to hide behind. Individual personalities were purposely stripped away, leaving only the strength of your own back bone and character. The military needed to make everyone the same, a blank canvas. Then begin the process of remolding. . . of brain washing. What a difference a day makes for the enlistee. After striping you down you get to meet a guy who is a copy of Clint Eastwood in Heartbreak Ridge, only meaner, uglier and louder. He comes in to test your resolve and your nerves. His sticks his ugly mug right in your grill and starts yelling so loud the windows crack. The air gets sucked right out of the room. It was amazing how many kids welted, cowered, how much of their strength was really associated with their own hair, beards, mustaches and raiment. It was a day everyone should experience once. A gut check. You see up front and personal what is left of an individual when all his or her personal props are removed. The military needs to erase the old before re-writing the new ..... compliments of Uncle Sam.

That first day was memorable. . . . a good time to pick out your boot camp buddies.

When you go into the first week of boot camp they give everyone the same physical fitness test, in this case six events all done in an hour. Each event was worth a hundred points. This physical part was right in my wheel house and I managed a perfect six hundred, then was told it was a first for the Coast Guard. So that night our company commander asked about the guy who scored 600 and I proudly stepped forward. It felt like he expected some big muscular dude, one he could proudly show off to the other companies. Instead he was looking at a rather scrawny 5'9" light weight with no visible muscles. He gave me a nod and that was it. But the next day during the morning grinder I detected a slight smile before the usual 'down for 50.' At that time I could do over a hundred push-ups in one minute so the physical part of military duty came pretty easy.

Later that first week we were taken out for training drills (the grinder) with rifles. The first hour a group of three very tall well-dressed dudes were watching 64 of us try to move rifles around and damn if that trio didn't come my way first. I was wondering what I had done wrong? The tallest of the trio looked down at me and asked, "Where'd you learn to handle that rifle boy?" "Sir, don't know nothing about this rifle, sir." True. He insisted I had been practicing and then asked if I would like to be part of the Honor Guard? That had a nice ring to it. . . and these guys were sporting leggings, ascots and cool uniforms, especially compared to our boot camp crap. So I said 'sir, yes sir', then he asked how tall I was. The three guys were all 6'3"- 6' 6" so tall was obviously important. I puffed up my 5'9" frame, looked the guy square in the chest and loudly said 6 feet, sir! He questioned that so I dropped it down to 5'11" and after he questioned that I dropped it down another inch. Anyway, he told me when and where to report for training and into the Honor Guard I went, so long boot camp. . . . after only a week.

The Honor Guard made me shoes with 3 inch soles and I was placed in the back of a line among 12 others that went from tallest to shortest. Our little 12 pack spent days learning to flip, twirl and toss rifles and after two weeks we were sent out to march in holiday parades and other local events, including the half time show at the East West Shrine Game in what was then called Kezar Stadium. I guess that was in 1964. While we were out there playing with rifles and having fun far away from Alemeda Island, the rest of those boys were going through hell, ie., boot camp. This was another dose of serendipity. But over confidence can lead to trouble. At the base I started sneaking out at night and going over to the movie house, restricted for officers only, leaving the enlisted barracks, crossing base camp and easing into the back row of the theater minutes after the movie started and then easing out minutes before it ended. In the dark no one was the wiser until one night some comedy film got me laughing so hard (a horrible he-haw donkey laugh) that one of the officers called me out. It took a lot of extra push ups, paint duty and some abuse to appease that mess, still I started to think of myself as Lucky Luke, bullet proof.

After six weeks it was out of boot camp, meaning the Honor Guard, and into active duty on the Coast Guard Cutter Dexter, 311 feet of old iron with a crew of 176 men. A friend passed me on the gang way as I was embarking and told me to go for the laundry room so I passed this hot tip on a Texan buddy and we both volunteered for laundry duty. . . . . for 176 men! Sounds like a mistake, like my luck had finally run out. Not so. The friend was dead right. . . for two reasons. When at sea, it sucked, rolling over waves trying to wash stacks of clothing, then ironing those uniforms with a big steam press that was maneuvered up and down by foot. But we were seldom at sea and it was the only duty that was given every night off, even officers did not get that. When we finished the work, the Texan and I were off to San Francisco in my Sprite which was parked only a hundred meters from the ship at the Alameda Base, and while in port no one brought us their dirty uniforms, not with a more professional free laundry on base.

Life on the Dexter was pretty mundane save for the 'Jelly Roll Thieves'. Turned out that in our sleeping quarters was a huge freezer bolted to the floor between a rows of bunks. This box had a double iron bar crossing the top locked at both ends, and was loaded with ice cream. The iron bars were loose, enough so that my bunk mate and I could pull one side up while the other reached in and grabbed a jelly roll, which we did every night after lights out. We both had strong skinny arms. The jelly rolls steadily declined, becoming ever more difficult to reach. One night while in port, actually in Eureka, it was my turn to reach in and his turn to hold up the bar. Suddenly the officer on duty came strolling into our dark sleeping quarters while my arm was fully extended into the freezer. The guy drops the bar and jumps back into his bunk. Caught like a rat in a frozen trap. I start sending out loud barfing noises, moaning and telling the duty officer to not get any closer, puke was all over the deck, that he should go grab a bucket and mop. He asks how could I possibly be seasick with the ship still in port, tied to the dock? Hmmm.

Good question? Moan louder. . . .

Luckily he reversed direction in search of a mop. It was too dark for him to see who was making all the noise and once gone, I call for help. The buddy (no more) jumps down, pulls up the iron bar and out comes a frozen jelly roll attached to a frozen arm. The last of our midnight snacks.

There were other cute moments like jumping ship and having to pay off the guy on night duty with a case of beer. Then tossing a bucket of oil down the side of the Dexter while in port just as a gust of wind came up, splattering black oil across a 10 foot swath of a pure white vessel. It took two fellow seamen holding my ankles, swinging me back and forth like a windshield wiper with oil rags in each hand, attempting to clean the side of a ship hanging upside down 14 feet above the dock. Another guy helped by going down the gangway to attack the oil splatter from below with Ajax, a bucket of water and a mop. Amazingly no officer came along to notice the slight color change before nightfall. At dawn we set sail out of Eureka Harbor before anyone saw the stain. Ahhhh, another dash of foolishness goes unpunished. More serendipity.

Let the games begin. After three months we walk off the Dexter at Alameda and we're all given credit slips worth the amount of money it would take each of us to get our preassigned destinations, for me a bus ride North 250 miles up the California coast to Eureka (Humboldt County). It was time for that "duration of your military obligation" to begin. Time for six years in purgatory. Instead of going north I got in my car and headed due south down Hwy. 101. When I got to So Cal I met up with a friend, bought a case of beer and headed out to the desert, to Palm Springs. What next? I did not relish living in Humboldt County, though it was the area or county my brother and his wife loved most on this planet. I liked the Redwoods but had something warmer and more exotic in mind. So after a few beers I drove over to the College of the Desert in Palm Springs and went into the Administration Building wearing my white Coast Guard uniform. Looking and feeling pretty good. I went up to a pretty young lady at the front desk and asked if she would be interested in helping me beat Uncle Sam? She laughed and said... how? I explained what I needed, and she said why not? Vietnam was a very unpopular war. I took out my orders and asked if she could re-type the form leaving certain lines blank. She agreed and half hour later I was back checking her fine work, the new unfinished orders. I then asked if she could ditto copy about 20 of these new orders, which she did, and last I asked if I could borrow her type writer.

I had to change the dates of discharge as well as the districts. The 11th district included San Francisco as well as Humboldt County. The 14th district was Hawaii. The dates and districts were changed and I thanked the lovely lady, found my friend and what was left of the beer, and off we drove back across the desert, this time to Norton Air Force Base. This was once a logistics depot and heavy-lift transport facility which included a variety of military aircraft. I was looking for a possible MAC flight to Hawaii, "military flights for military personnel." We get to Norton and I walk my Lilly white uniform into a huge hanger dotted with nothing but blue Air Force colors, mixed with a few green and brown Marines. You think my Coast Guard whites stuck out? I headed for a desk in front of some Air Force officer sporting more strips than a zebra, perhaps a Chief Master Sergeant. He looked at me like a Martian, then asked what I was doing there and what planet I came from? I explain I was in the Coast Guard Reserves and looking for a MAC flight to Hawaii, then reluctantly handed him my false orders. He declared he had never seen a Coast Guard uniform at his base before, that I looked odd. Really! This officer was especially curious about my seeking a MAC flight to Hawaii? He asked why I came to Norton and glances at my orders. My knees are knocking. This could be a serious mistake. He says he needs to check out the orders and disappears for about 10 minutes. By then a diaper was needed. I was really torn between running out to the parking lot or holding my ground. The old saying, 'go big or go home.' But home in this case was a military brig. Retreat was not an option with him holding my name on false orders. When he came back he repeats how odd all this looks and then points to the very last line on the orders, lucky number 13.

It reads, "Transportation to be paid for by self." Short and to the point, what point?

I ask what the problem is and he asks how I plan to pay for a military flight? I said I wasn't, it was being paid for by the Coast Guard. He points to line 13 again, the one stating "paid for by self" meaning on my dime. He explains flights out of Norton are not commercial. Military only. Gives me the evil eye.

Would I be in front of a firing squad by morning? I then mention the credit slip given to me by the Coast Guard, the pink one. . . . the one outside in my car. That credit slip was of course for a bus ride to Humboldt County from Alameda, not a flight to Hawaii from Norton AFB, especially not a military flight. He suggests I fetch that credit slip asap. I turn to go but have the wits to calmly take my false orders out of his hand. Fortunately my friend and the car are still there, less two beers. My buddy mentions I look as white as the uniform, and asks what happened? He doesn't notice the soil mark on my pant leg. Before the question gets answered we are gone. . . . headed back toward the Pacific Coast. Shit, I if I could get that close with a Chief Master Sergeant in the Air Force at Norton then LAX should be easy. So it's over to LAX the next day, white uniform, soiled mark removed, false orders, and a surf board under my arm. Those orders earned me a nice half price one way military discounted ticket, $50! This was the 60's. So off to the 14th Coast Guard District on a commercial flight I go. . . off to the Aloha state.

The day after landing in Honolulu it was time to face the music, to report to Coast Guard Headquarters. As I no longer could hand over false orders, I give my original orders to some guy sitting at a desk with a rank of seaman, and he takes a long lingering look, trying to figure out what the hell he is holding? He notices the orders indicate I am two days AWOL, (Absent Without Official Leave) as well as 3,000 miles from where I belong, that being Northern California (Humboldt County). As best I can recall he looks up and mentions both mistakes and asks what the hell I am doing in Hawaii? I tell him I had to make some hard choices, Hawaii or Humboldt? Where would he rather spend six years of this life? He looks at me, laughs and says, you either are the dumbest SOB on the planet. . . or you have balls made of brass. He suggests they will likely feed me to the sharks or toss me in the brig, but complimented me on my choice of real estate. . . . and wished me luck. Lots of it. Luck, or perhaps that other word. . . . serendipity?

I regret that I will never know what the Coast Guard brass thought or said the moment they looked at my orders? Obviously someone in command had a sense of humor, or just decided it wasn't worth sending me back to California. Fortunately I did not get tossed into the brig. Military prisons are no joke. A couple days later I was informed about my transfer, and thus began my new life in our 50th state.

It does not take long to make Hawaii your home. Ask any tourist who has stayed longer than a month. Everyone soon picks up some pidgen English, Hawaiian style, speaking 'da kind', and to use the common hand signal to greet others, the "shaka, brah!" The beaches, palm trees and Hawaiian music welcome everyone.

It was the 60's and I was just another Haole trying to adapt to the Aloha spirit and find some kind of work that would allow me to survive in paradise while I served out my time in the Coast Guard. As mentioned, this was before aids and before plastic surgery, saline and silicone. People were still in pretty good shape, not packing Big Mac bodies into bikinis. What you saw was what you got, real and not well hidden. Never will there be another period like the sixties; the diversity, conflicts, hope and anger. No cellphones. Most recall it as a time of sex, drugs, rock and roll music, and revolutionary thoughts. Everyone was stoned, surfing, or screwing on a daily basis all while enjoying the natural and human scenery. A mix of metaphysics and idealistic love.

It was pretty crazy and if there was a summer of love to be enjoyed, then why not in the state of endless summers? I was soon out on bikini patrol along the shores of Waikiki keeping the occasional eye out for enemy periscopes to fulfill my duties with the Coast Guard. Jobs were everywhere as were the ladies. Soon I found work as the rotating manager at four wonderful restaurants right on the corner of the Market Place, fronting Kalakaua Avenue. My little apt. was over on Kuhio Avenue, one block away. The four places I worked for back then were called Gauguins, Tahiti By Six, The Canton Puka and Christopher's. Not only are all these restaurants now gone, so is The Market Place as of 2014.

Nothing stays the same for long in Hawaii, but those 7 years were the best, most uninhibited, carefree and fun loving years of my entire life. Memories still linger. Life was shameless, a mixture of ladies and beaches and constant sunshine. The girls were mostly tourists who came to visit the islands for one or two weeks, looking to escape routines and responsibilities back home, their jobs and relationships or just bad weather. Two weeks to get brown and beautiful and celebrate the reckless idealism of youth. Providing a joyful experience to those millions of tourists was a full time job for residents, Haole, Hapa Haole and locals alike, all competing for the chance to entertain the rotation of bodies flying in daily. For me it required a lot of trips over to the North Shore, a drive I called 'the brown bag express'. A bottle of wine, plastic cups, some chips and sunscreen tossed into a paper bag. The rest was a blend of bikinis and beaches . . . usually over near Laie or out Makaha way. It was tough work but someone had to do it. It was personal, double duty, serving our tourist industry as well as our country.

An added bonus for working in those four restaurants was getting to listen to the Joey Buskin Trio at Gauguins. Joey was an American Jazz Pianist who stopped traffic on Kalakaua at the Market Place every night, in fact nearly everyone that came to Hawaii came to Waikiki and the Market Place to hear good music, eat good food and meet good people. A few names who came to listen to Joey Buskin while I was there was Jonathan Winters, Ray Anthony, Lou Rawls, Lee Marvin, Pat Boone, James Garner, Zsa Zsa Gabor, and probably dozens of other celebrities I did not recognize.

What does this have to do with the Coast Guard? One of the district commanders came to Gauguin's one night and I made sure he got the best seat in the house. It helped convince him, and therefore the

Coast Guard, that I was a legit part of a family that owned restaurants all over the USA and that it was eventually going to be necessary for me to leave the islands in order to help with the family business. . . . restaurants! In other wards it was time to use up a few of those blank orders that were ditto copied for me back at the College of the Desert in Palm Springs. The commander signed off on my leaving the 14th district (Hawaii) for some months and so I packed my uniforms and was gone. The first order was legit as I recall, from the 14th district back to the 11th which included Los Angeles. After that I would have to use the blank orders if I did not want to fly commercially, if I did not want to pay. So the first false order would be tested at the Van Nuys Air National Guard Base which was a former US Air Force Base. I was hoping to find a flight Eastward. That base was home to some big bellied C-97 cargo aircraft which could also carry 10 passengers. First come, first serve. I told them I was headed for New York and showed them my orders (false). They allowed me to jump a flight headed for Dover Air Force Base in the state of Delaware. It was a nervous moment, but actually proved quite easy. The problem was I also had no service ID. I lost my ID card back in Hawaii on some beach. But they never even asked. My white uniform, military haircut and the false orders were good enough. Lucky Luke was part of the cargo headed East. There were ten of us on that flight, our ten bunks anchored to the deck of the cargo plane, but no one slept. Our little group played poker most of the flight which allowed me to travel from Manhattan Beach, California to Manhattan Island, New York, actually making 50 cents in the process. I had won about $12 bucks playing poker which paid for a hamburger, beer, phone call and bus ride to NYC with 50 cents left over. One of the lowest fares ever coast to coast. I eventually crossed the states at least 7 times, once on a bicycle, but never made money doing it. The 'one way u-drive cars and RV's' I later drove all over the states included gas, but I had to pay for food and drink.

After New York I recall checking into some Coast Guard base over in Connecticut. Being in the reserves requires spending one week end per month on active duty. So I check into this base on a Saturday morning wearing my nice white uniform, which turned out to be the only white uniform on the base, sort of like back at Norton AFB. Dark blue was the common color of choice for the Coast Guard along the Eastern

Seaboard. Once again I stood out like a penguin at a turkey trot. Things at that base started badly and quickly deteriorated. The week-end I arrived got hit with an unannounced base inspection by some district commander. There I was, one white uniform in a crowd of blue and some commander unexpectedly arrives and is now walking down each line doing a dress code check. When he gets to me he does a double take, smiles and asks where I'm from? I say Hawaii, just visiting for the week-end. All went well until I'm sitting in some classroom afterward and a guy walks in looking for the new visitor in white, saying the base officer wanted to see me. That officer asks me 'why I am there' and I do my best to explain. Not easy. He then asks for my service ID. I explain how I lost it in Hawaii. He asks why he should believe me... and then mentions how strange that I should show up just when his base gets hit with an unannounced inspection? He actually believes I might be a spy, perhaps planted there and he does not want me on the base. So they decide to send me out to the guard shack or gate a hundred yards away from the buildings, to separate me from all other humans. My instructions are to stop all incoming traffic and check ids.

I am now a sentry. . . . isolated and harmless. Ha, ha. The first car pulls up, a station wagon. The driver is in civies, his young son sitting next to him.

I ask for his ID. He yells WHAT!! . . . and not in a polite way? I try again and he gets really irritated. He then asks who I think I am talking to? I say I have no idea. He loudly explains that he is the base commander, another one! (How many commanders can one base have?) I apologize, and explain I have to check his ID anyway. Commanders of bases don't get asked. He is now pissed and asks to see my ID. Ooooops, wrong question. You can imagine what follows. He guns the station wagon across the base and within minutes some guy is running back out to the guard gate. More good news. . . . they want to see me... again!! This could have gone very badly (you think?) but instead they just shut me down for the week-end. Tell me to leave, get lost!! You can see why I began to think I was bullet proof. Serendipity? Yes! It was time to fill out another false order, find another air force base, another C-97 (pretty sure that was the plane), and this I did...

just in time to for the Mardi Gras. . . in 1968. . . in New Orleans. My first and last.

The Mardi Gras is a fun two weeks filled by thousands of loud and drunk humans breaking rules, bones and sound barriers. . . . enjoying an annual celebration accentuated by costumes, beads, parades, floats, dancing girls, crowds and endless music, much of it along Bourbon Street. I soon hook up with a lovely lady visiting from New York City who just happens to have a nice hotel room right on Bourbon Street. The perfect start to any Mardi Gras. I recall little of that week but there was this young black kid who asked us for some coin, then told us he knew or was related to Otis Redding. Before we donated to his musical career we asked for him to prove this relationship to Otis so he did a version of "Sittin' On the Dock of the Bay" that was amazing. That boys' dancing and singing stopped everyone, filled hearts which in turn filled his pockets.

After that there was a party some stranger invited us to. The party was in a nice hotel but it turned out to be an orgy. . . . for me another first. . . and last. Kind of bizarre and quirky. . . . or kinky. We found the hotel room on the second floor and walked in. It took a few minutes to realize what was going on and as we were about to make our exit when one of naked ladies from the orgy stood up, strolled past us out the door and down the balcony walkway into another party, this one filled with well-dressed couples, like a frat party. She went to the middle of the room surrounded by at least twenty people, stood there butt naked for some minutes before a pair of gawking guys got nudged by their embarrassed dates to do something. One of the boys took off his suit coat, covered her and then guided her back to the room with the orgy. Neither room offered our kind of fun, but it did make our Mardi Gras more memorable.

Next thing I recall was being with Ms. New York in that great hotel room on Bourbon Street. While testing the mattresses the doorbell rang and it was the hotel manager wanting to know if she happened to have any unregistered guest in her room? I drop between the beds under some sheets and tried to vanish. He wants me out within the hour. The next day she tells me the real reason he wanted me out was because he wanted in. . . . he returned minutes after I exited. Room service at its finest. While it was unsavory, I did appreciate his taste in women, so much so that after the Mardi Gras and before going back to Hawaii I changed plans and planes and headed north up to the Big Apple for another round of what we started on Bourbon Street. This detour was on my own dime. No false orders.

A friend I met in New Orleans drove me out to the Louis Armstrong International Airport for my departure. Inside while buying a ticket to New York I noticed everybody turning their heads staring at someone. That someone was a beautiful black lady wearing an all-white dress walking through the airport with her mother. Gorgeous! Reminded me of a young Diana Ross. Long curly black hair, petite, stunning. I fetch my ticket to LaGuardia Airport in Queens, NYC and then we went looking for a bite of food. The airport restaurant had a nice hostess and I explained to her my issue with digesting food when not looking at something beautiful and then I point to a cute girl seated at the counter.

She said she could do one better and actually takes us to an attached dining area where that lovely black lady is sitting with her mother. We are placed at the table next to them and I thanked her for her excellent taste. While eating I overhear that this black girl is also flying into LaGuardia on the same Delta Flight and then we all find out via the airport speaker system that our departure has been delayed an hour. That's good. Time for some fun, time to try and meet the lady in white that was turning heads. My friend wishes me luck and heads back to New Orleans. I now have an hour to play with. This was not just another bikini on a Waikiki beach. Much more complicated. I seat myself behind her and her Mom in the huge waiting lounge and make a plan. Then I try to locate some guy to aid in the sting. I find a young man standing alone who looks approachable, say hello and eventually point to the lady I am hoping to meet and he says, "you and every other guy in the airport." I ask, 'would he like to help?' 'Sure, why not?'

Here is what you need to say, but don't over play it. I will be sitting next to her Mom. You come over and ask, "Sorry to disturb, but I think I have seen you before out West. Don't you live in Brentwood or that area in California." 'Yes.' "Are you riding you motorcycle around Brentwood a lot?" 'Yes.' "In fact don't you sometimes ride with your brother. 'Yes. 'In fact isn't your brother Steve McQueen?" 'Yes.'(Back in Hawaii a couple tourists told me I looked a little like McQueen, visitors that were either intoxicated or trying to bribe me for a better seat at Gauguin's. . . still it had a nice ring to it.)

So the guy says he just wanted to shake my hand and off he went. Played like a pro, but the mother and daughter show nothing, no reaction. Bummer. The two young ladies on the other side of the bench overheard every word and timidly come around to ask for an autograph. . . . compliments of Chad McQueen! Sure. No problem.

Nothing came from that first try save for my new name, and two autographs. Next idea. I go off to the information counter where I explain my plight to a nice lady behind the desk, point to the black beauty in the white dress, and ask for her help. Will she send out an announcement over the airport paging system? She agrees and I hustle back to my spot with the ladies on the bench. Out of the speakers comes, "long distance telephone call for Chad McQueen please at the information counter", which she repeats. Off I go to thank the lady at the information counter over a good laugh. She wishes me well. . . and back I go. Nothing much happens other than a few words with the mother. By then our flight is nearing departure so I go back to the information counter and ask the lady for one last try. By this time our flight and gate have been announced and we are all headed down the hall when another blast comes through the airport speakers, "phone call for Chad McQueen please, at the information counter." Repeat. The Mom and daughter look at me as I turn to go and Mom says, 'these people just won't leave you alone, will they?' Progress! I smile, run back for another thanks and laugh with information lady and quickly reverse to the departure gate. When I get there the lovely black lady who has shown nothing, comes straight over and puts her arm in my arm and asks if I wouldn't mind escorting her onto the plane because some guys were tailgating her. Touchdown!

We both say good bye to her Mom who lives in New Orleans and we board the plane. As we enter the aircraft everyone greets this beautiful lady by her first name. Robbie. It's my time to wonder? It turns out she was an air hostess working for Delta and now was dead heading back to her place in NYC. Once on the plane she asked me what all that fuss was about back in the airport? I play down the part about being Steve McQueen's brother and we end up sharing a wonderful few hours before landing at La Guardia. Ebony and ivory.

The connection continues right on into her little apt. in the Big Apple for the night. As it turns out she is also connected to the leading ground gainer for the Jets (no need to mention names) and so I am up and out before the first editions of the New York Times hit the sidewalks. But it was all good, going from the most beautiful black women I had ever met to that lady from Bourbon Street who escorted me to the orgy, admired my disappearing act in her hotel room, danced with me on Bourbon Street and shared that great version of "Sittin' On The Dock Of The Bay". She was the main attraction in the Big Apple anyway, and our reunion did not disappoint.

The old saying,'no effort, no reward'. So true. This was gain without pain.

After a few days in NYC it was time for one more false order and another MAC flight out of the same Dover Air Force Base in Delaware, this time headed West to California and on to Hawaii. I recall being allowed to sit in the cockpit of that C-97 with the pilots during the flight and that first great look at the Rocky Mountains from above. So after crossing the states in both directions mostly with MAC flights using up about five false orders, going to New York, Connecticut, New Orleans, and places in between, I was once again back on bikini patrol, developing eye strain and trying not to trip over those Au Naturale bumps lining the artificial sands of Waikiki. Sharing those seven years and hundreds of trips to the North Shore would fill any dairy. The sixties were 'the summers of love'. . . a time of crazy passion, of youth and innocence, of wild and wonderful music (The Moody Blues, The Doors, Pink Floyd, The Who, Simon & Garfunkel, Mamas and the Papas, Crosby, Stills, Nash and Young, John Mayall,the list is long) and our apartments decorated with 'India Imports' cloth, candles and aromatic incense. Most humans were breathing in a whole lot of strange biotic material a bit stronger than incense. Everyone and everything was getting high, loaded and laid. During the 60's there was a downside in Waikiki as well, too much development and construction, something that has never stopped since Hawaii became a state back in 1959. . . and especially in Honolulu where the 'lift crane' was chosen the new state bird. Dozens of long necked construction cranes stood high above the rising and spreading city skyline. The actual state bird, the Nene, was nearly as extinct as was public access to beach front property. Hawaii was being bought, sold, paved, developed and changed as fast as a fashion show model changes outfits. By the 70's the Hawaiians had lost a large portion of the most valuable part of their culture, their land! Hawaii was quickly going beneath the wheel of progress, everything sacrificed or bulldozed for the all mighty tourist dollar.

The Lyrics in 'Big Yellow Taxi' by Joni Mitchell said it perfectly.

"They paved paradise and put up a parking lot, with a pink hotel, a boutique and a swinging hot spot.

Don't it always seem to go that you don't know what you've got Till it's gone.

They paved paradise. And put up a parking lot. . . ."

It was time to try another part of our planet less exploited, an urge that was expedited by the Coast Guard Reserve Unit I was still in. One of the local warrant officers grew weary of my antics and suggested to the chain of command that I should be made an example of by activating me and literally shipping me off to Vietnam. It was time to punish their non-conformist. Through the grape vine word reached me that I was about to get reassigned. . . . to Southeast Asia. Once again, 'desperate times called for desperate measures.' It was necessary to get sick, in this case something serious enough to get me kicked out of the Coast Guard, something like a good old case of scoliosis. (Severe curvature of the spine.) After sifting through a medical book, it seemed like any spine could have an abnormal curvature, especially one banged around by so many different sports. The idea came from having a bad mouth. . . . well not in the way you might think. As mentioned, my Mother worked as a dental hygienist, a place I visited often due to being blessed with more than my fair share of cavities. All those visits to the dentist required x-rays. . . . and in my case the radiation did me more good than harm. I noticed that whomever and whenever X-rays were taken, the person doing it always stepped out of the room, then pushed some button. It was time to bet my future on that observation but first I needed to prove to the Coast Guard that my scoliosis was for real. It took a couple of visits to the medical center and enough complaining about lower pack spasms, stiffness, numbness, shooting leg pain, and headaches, all of which is easy to fake, to convince the staff I needed X-rays! After the interviews I got my appointment. Once in the medical center I was asked to strip down to my skivvies and then placed on a cold table. The medical officer in charge placed me in three different positions, both sides and on my back. After each position he would step out of the room and zap me. Bada bing-bada bang-bada boom. As soon as he disappeared I crunched my lower vertebrates together so hard I farted a few times. I squeezed down on the muscles in my lower back until it actually hurt. .. it still does. My farts and back parts were now on film and they said it would be about a week before the results were available. During that week while sitting on a beach in Waikiki I just happened to see the kid that sat at the front desk at the Coast Guard Med Center. I went over and said hello and when he recognized me he mentioned something about my bad back. He just let it slip out. I asked how he knew this. He told me that my back was so bad the technician who took the x-rays shared them with the entire office staff, showing everyone the lovely curvature in my lower spine. He said my back was nearly L shaped. He apologized for telling me this as it was actually private medical information. While my insides jumped for joy, my facial expression got as long as an Airedale terrier. . . . death in paradise! So he tries to cheer me up by saying this could be my liberation day, that get out of jail freedom card. I was ecstatic, euphoric, elated, but could not show any of that outwardly. By telling me these results he was allowing me to return to the Medical Center knowing what cards the Coast Guard held. I was playing with a stacked deck, no more lost sleep, breathing suddenly became easier. A week later they called me in for the results, sat me down and informed me I was unfit for active duty. The medical officer assured me scoliosis like mine could be corrected by a good orthopedic surgeon. He handed me my discharge papers and wished me well. My six years in the reserves just got cut in half and that potential holiday to Vietnam canceled. Hawaii had been great, but it was time to celebrate the next three years of freedom elsewhere.

After a back flip in the parking lot, I drove my little sports car over to Waikiki giving silent thanks to all those dentists, those x-rays. . . . . to serendipity.

There was a slight epidemic of scoliosis in that Coast Guard district shortly after my release. A couple of reserve buddies came by for drinks while taking a few notes. It was time to get off bikini patrol, stop straining my eyes over all those beautiful bodies. There were still a few blank orders, one of which was filled out to help snag another MAC flight to Boston on my way to Europe. It was in Boston where I parted ways with my white Coast Guard uniform. This strange journey all started with that pretty young girl at the College of the Desert in Palm Springs? She really did help me beat Uncle Sam. It ended with one of those well-endowed bikinis I had met in Waikiki who was now living in Boston. My time in the Coast Guard turned into three of the best years of my life, nothing but positive lessons, one being how to enjoy the service without really trying.

I saw much more of the USA than the average Coast Guard reservist, got to march in parades, enjoy the Mardi Gras, stay in great shape, even learn a little discipline which I now try to pass along to my daughter. Beside the ladies, memories and sunsets, Hawaii offered water skiing, volleyball, months of marlin fishing on the Kona Coast, the art of being a waiter, opening wine and talking trash or 'da kind' with people from all parts of the globe. Those uninhibited years in Hawaii were a nice prelude to the 30 plus years of travel that would follow.

Regretfully I have yet to visit Vietnam.

"SLEEPING WITH THE DOGS" -
III
NINE CAT LIVES

The nine cat lives. . . these nine lives are really a myth related to a cat's ability to always land on their feet. Escaping death is a form of landing on your feet vs. landing six feet under. All of us come close to dying before we actually do. How close is filled with speculation and often prone to exaggeration. When your heart stops on the operating table or you are a cancer survivor or survive any kind of bad accident, you have landed on your feet and get to go on with life. . . . . a good feeling, even for cats. I believe in the old adage that says, "We do not really get close to life until we get close to death." This is not referring to old age, but rather to any near death experience.

The following pages relate the top nine times in my personal life when I landed on my feet. How close I came to landing six feet under will remain unknown.

1 – The Golden Triangle, Burma. First to lay a little foundation.

A year earlier on a sandy shore in Laguna Beach I ran into a nice looking blond in one of those bikinis. Her body and mind were as prone to being both curious and restless as were mine, so I asked if she might be interested in doing some traveling? Sure she said, 'where do you want to go?' After more conversation I suggested a trip around the world. A home run or nothing. 'Why not?' So we both quit our meager jobs, put our meager funds together, stuffed our meager back packs with meager belongings and a month later off we went. The end result of that chance meeting (serendipity) on a beach in Laguna turned into 19 months of adventure travel around the globe during which we spent 25 hours a day and 8 days a week together. Her name was Donna. It turned out to be one hell of a first date! Total time spent together would probably equal about 13 years of marriage. It wasn't what one would call a romantic journey as much as a survival test. Our adventure connected us to the world and me to the camera. The 18,000 photos I would take with an old Nikon F allowed me to step into that circle of professional photography, a profession that has since paid all the bills and opened all the doors to the world. That first date with Donna turned into a game changer. After our journey I would forever be able to go to work loving what I did. No more time clocks or working for others. I would hence forth become the essence of a freelance photographer. A keen eye was always necessary while on bikini patrol in Waikiki and again that day in Laguna Beach, and now that eye was connected to a camera. A match that would subsidize my curiosity and last a lifetime!

Our first four months were spent traveling around Europe followed by three months in Africa and then a full year in various parts of Asia, a few weeks of which were in the country I most prefer for its culinary offerings, Thailand. While in Thailand we headed up north to the city of Chiang Mai, "The Rose of the North". Colorful umbrellas were everywhere. After checking into a small hotel we went in search of some trekking company, one that could take us up into the Golden Triangle. We wanted to visit a few of those Hill Tribes, something thousands of tourists were doing even while being warned not to by embassies and consulates. It was still pretty wild in those parts. A sign over one of the trekking outfits caught our attention. "If you see another tourist on your trek we will fully refund your money." Perfect! The great escape. After a six pack of tourists were signed up, we were introduced to our young Thai guide and then driven by pickup truck to the small town of Fang in the northern most part of Chiang Mai Province. This is about as near to the top of Thailand as you can get, close to Burma (now called Myanmar) and part of that infamous Golden Triangle. We learn from our small Thai guide that we will be crossing a stream about 20 times the first day. No rain, so not much water. That first night we slept in some remote hill tribe village, ate sitting on the floor of a hut and reveled in our natural mountain high. After dinner Donna and I went out for a stroll among the village huts. It was dusk and we noticed two guys talking, one carrying a military rifle, a semi-automatic with a clip. Not the typical village hunting rifle but so what. It was an old guy talking with some kid holding his M-1 carbine. The next morning our six pack is feeling higher than the jungle canopy, meandering slowly through lush green vegetation while singing any tune that came into our six different heads. We were feeling euphoric, on the loose and bullet proof. For hours we mixed our favorite songs with the indigenous birds. It was all perfect until three young guys stepped out of the thick brush ahead, one with that military M-1 rifle we saw the night before. Our group greeted this trio of locals feeling upbeat and talkative, maybe a bit too talkative. The Thai guide wasn't smiling and in his broken English told us to shut up. This gang of kids wasn't there to welcome us. The one with the M-1 started pointing it our way. The mood changed and the Thai guide seemed to be begging for his life, crying, sweating, and arms up. We learned later that most Hill Tribe people hate Thais for burning their opium crops, destroying their livelihoods. So the kid with the M-1 walks up to our guide, puts the point of the barrel to his forehead and pulls the trigger. Shit! Instead of brains the bullet parts his hair thanks to another bandit. One of the other guys raised the rifle just as it was fired. The Thai kid is shitting in his pants and I'm a foot away, doing the same.

Our gang of happy hikers is no longer euphoric. We are directed at gunpoint to get down on the ground. Suddenly this huge vast jungle feels like a silent green graveyard, the absolute middle of nowhere. The guy with the rifle is jacked up on something, looking anxious to unload the rest of the clip. We no longer feel like bullet proof tourists. All of us sensed this could end badly. Would they rape the two women or just take our belongings and then blow us away? Who would ever know if they put a bullet in each of us and left us as fodder for wildlife or to just rot away? We went through some serious anxious moments, everyone keeping their heads down, not daring to look at their three faces. They then started to unload our bags and backpacks, taking nearly all our belongings including Donna's lovely underwear. (Later I would try to visualize what her bras and panties would look like on those hill tribe women?) When they grabbed my camera and film I cringed, and then when they took my exposed film, my future, I looked up and said out loud, not the film! The rifle was pointed right at my head and looking at me was that kid in the village from the night before. The tourist next to me whispered from ground level, 'let it go'. . . . . and I did. Thus I can now write about it. I can also wonder what I lost on those exposed rolls of film. Film can be replaced but not the images. . . . and not our lives. After taking as much as they could carry, including our shoes, we waited for that clip to be unloaded into us. . . but instead they quietly vanished back into the jungle. It had taken a day and a half of casual trekking to get to that point. After gathering what was left of our gear and wits, we headed back barefoot, covering the same distance and stream crossings in just 6 hours. Fear and adrenaline kept us moving.

Once back to Fang the guide and other four tourists were taken back to Chiang Mai. Donna and I stayed behind in the village for the night, our second worst decision in Thailand. We did this because I had lost valuable items, camera, lenses, tripod and film, plus we were the only two people who actually saw the bandits. We knew they were connected (in cahoots) with that old man from the village we slept at and we wanted to be sure the police understood this. As it turned out after listing the value of all stolen items on a report at the small Fang police station, (slightly padded for insurance reasons) the chief of police started focusing more on the dollar amounts of what we had lost than the robbers. The chief saw us as bloody rich tourists who needed to be robbed. . . . . By police, not bandits! Luckily all of us had been instructed to leave our money, tickets and passports back in our Chiang Mai hotels. The police chief now wanted to know where those items were. He was not concerned that we actually knew who robbed us or about some old villager. The police would have preferred owning what we listed as lost, not chasing the ones who had taken it through some jungle, possibly getting killed for their efforts. The local police earned only a few bucks a month and were not exactly in love with tourists. We started to freak out sensing this could get worse, knowing we had already passed up our only safe passage out of Fang. We were stuck in this lawless place for the night. Once again serendipity stepped forward in the form of some Dutch guy who was living in Fang with his Thai wife. As I am part Dutch, it was only right to be helped by a compatriot. He took us to his place for the night and later shared stories of how local police dealt with bandits..... by cutting their heads off, then mounting those heads on shafts in front of the police station. They added that even a police chief had recently been shot, that no one was really safe this far north. The next morning they pointed us to a back alley that lead to the bus station and we jumped the first bus heading south to Chiang Mai. Still we were pretty nervous as our Dutch host also mentioned bandits stopping buses, boarding and then robbing people.... or worse. Actually the bus did stop and guess who got on..... yep, the guy who held the M-1 on us in the jungle. He sat right across the aisle from me and after I pointed him out to Donna neither of us breathed all the way to Chiang Mai. I am pretty sure it was not the same guy, but....? By now we were really nervous and gun-shy.... literally!!

The day after we got back to Chiang Mai the local newspaper included a short article about six tourists getting robbed in a jungle near Fang. It was our six pack of idiots. Bad news travels fast, even in Northern Thailand. Everything in the article was pretty accurate save for the spelling of our names and for that reason I think no one bothered to pick up a souvenir copy. We were all just glad to still be absorbing oxygen.

2 – Running the Colorado River through the Grand Canyon -

As this little episode was already included in one of my books titled, "Through the Grand Canyon", I will just borrow a page from that book.

I now have 11 photography books in print, none of which would exist if any of these episodes, or cats, had not survived.

Back in the 80's I was lucky enough to know Martin Litton who was the owner/operator of the Grand Canyon Dory Company, a great American and a man who helped save the Grand Canyon from getting submerged under water as was Glen Canyon by the Glen Canyon Dam. Glen Canyon now sleeps under Lake Powell, though perhaps not for long as the lake is slowly drying up, shrinking, making the dam ever more obsolete. Anyway, Martin allowed me three opportunities to ride in one of his many colorful dories through the Grand Canyon in exchange for photographs and the ecological work I was doing in Sweden. Each journey on the river took between 14 and 18 days and it was during the second dory trip that one of these life and death moments took place. On every run through the Grand Canyon one or more of the dories does flip, usually in some rapid where passengers and boat get transported down a long wet bumpy conveyor belt. It's cold, wild. . . . and memorable. But the flip I write about took place in a whirlpool below some no name rapid. Both my Irish girlfriend, Annie Donohoe, and I just happened to be in the same dory when things went wrong. I have since named that whirlpool, 'the Donohoe Dump!' Our dory came into the eddy below this small rapid sideways and the low gunnel dipped into the swirling pool, grabbing the oar out of Nels' (our boatman) hand creating a kind of fulcrum that pulled the side of our dory down into the whirlpool, sucking the boat over so fast that no one had the chance to jump out, all of us going directly under into an angry brown circle. As the boat went over I heard what sounded like a gunshot which later turned out to be the wooden oar splitting.

Everything went instantly black, from sitting on a boat to having it sitting on us, all of which was spinning. The whirlpool flushed us downward while the life jackets pulled us upward. Those of us who's life jackets won the tug of war were now pinned under a swirling metal deck, getting our heads banged around like pin balls, everyone searching for light and oxygen. Later we discovered that each of us thought they were the only unlucky one under the boat. We all experienced something similar but different, all thinking they had taken their last breath. It was determined later that Nels came up first, immediately crawling onto the bottom of the spinning boat in search of survivors. I was struggling like crazy to pull myself from under the boat, against the swirling water. In those long seconds I recall seeing a replay of my past life flashing by, milliseconds of images caused by panic and fear triggering excessive amounts of adrenaline into my brain cells. This just wasn't happening. From joy to panic in an instant. I felt angry, frustrated, scared. Life was not supposed to end this way. I pulled on one railing with all my strength, saw some light and jerked my head up for a quick gulp of air before the boat cracked my head, sliding back over me, pressing me back under the deck. I started to pass out when the "Ootsa Lake" finally spun out of the whirlpool allowing the river current to pull me free. Air! You forget just how important oxygen is until it's taken away. Once up I looked around for Annie. By that time the dory was already 50 feet upstream. A quick head count. Nels was on the capsized boat and another head was down river, Mary. I could not get back to the dory and I could not see Annie. I felt sick and scared and emotionally drained. It was not possible that anyone could still be under water and alive. My personal ordeal seemed like ten minutes, though probably closer to one. Annie was not comfortable being under water, in fact she hated it. When getting ready for this river trip we went down to the Laguna Beach shore to let her practice going beneath a few small waves. Her fear of water was born in childhood and for the wrong reasons. Her alcoholic Irish father had punished her as a child by pushing her head under water in the bathtub. She was terrified of water but she gave it a try, dipping quickly into each wave, trying to learn the difference between being below water and above, when to breathe in, when not to. Her longest held breath that morning was about 8 seconds. After half an hour she started to relax a bit. I promised her nothing ever happens on these river trips anyway. Wrong! The Colorado River had just swallowed five of us and only three were spit back out. I was sick with anger and fear and was just about to scream when Annie's head popped up right next to the capsized dory. Nels grabbed her and pulled her onto the bottom of the boat while it continued its slow journey downriver. Even from far away I could see red on the white wooden boat and knew it must be coming out of Annie's hard Irish head. But still there she was. Another missing head belonging to Patti was hidden behind the boat, so five bodies up, all cats accounted for, three with the dory and two floating freely. Far down river was Mary cruising along in her life jacket. Nels grabbed the flip lines and with the help of Patti and Annie got the Ootsa Lake righted, eventually floating down river to pluck me out and then Mary. All of us were bruised and in shock but the only blood visible was Irish. The side of Annie's face was red as was her shoulder but she was actually smiling. A tough beautiful bird, one I should never have let fly away. The other boats were already on shore down river, busy setting up camp when we pull in. No one had a clue what the five of us had just gone through. In fact the only indication was the blank looks on our faces and the blood on Annie's. We sat down drained of energy while the lead guide, Kenton, got out a medical kit. Annie's hair was too thick to cut away so instead they used her hair as best they could to tie off the scalp wound, then wrapped a huge bandage around her head and over her auburn locks. She now looked a little like an Irish Betsy Ross. In the flip we had lost a few hats, lotions and sunglasses but no cameras, and no lives. The next day we all shared our personal accounts on what happened, each of us offering a different version. No one knew the exact amount of time they were under water, but Mary was the first up describing how she was pulled to the bottom of the river by the whirlpool, then yanked right back up by her life jacket, free and clear of the boat. Annie and Patti were under the longest, the three of us pinned under the dory. Somehow Annie managed to stay calm during that extremely frightening ordeal, miraculously holding her breath for over a minute while getting her head kicked around by the metal deck. Ya gotta love the Irish for their spirit and hardheadedness. We all burned one of our nine cat lives that day. Luckily we all can now share that moment in every tomorrow.

3 – Skydiving in Hawaii. . . . or at least ski jumping from an airplane -

During this period I was living in the Islands and working with restaurants down in Waikiki. One of the many waiters I worked with was doing a bit of ski diving. He was always trying to convince me to give it a try. After several offers it seemed worth the time to at least go have a look so a girlfriend and I drove across Oahu to a small airfield where hang gliders and sky divers were doing their thing. Back then playing with danger was less regulated, so there was no need to sign legal waivers or liability papers, at least none that I recall. After a couple beers my friend convinced me to give it a go and then offered us a look at how they packed their own parachutes. . . . sheets, lines, good old tuck and roll. After that I got a quick briefing on safety and jumping. He had me stand on some picnic table and hop off backwards, arms out, body arched. Something about not wanting me to hit the tail wing when departing from the plane. Then the important points, the rip cords on the parachutes . . . and those handles that control flight left and right, the steering wheels. He was giving me the crash course (well, hopefully not) on sky diving and unfortunately, precious little of what he said registered in my nervous brain.

I just wanted to go up, then down. So he put a couple of parachutes on me, big one in back, little one in front . . . and explained why two chutes. It was important to know what to do should the first parachute tangle. He said that from my low altitude jump there would be about 10–15 seconds to escape a tangled back chute, then pull the release on the front chute. He added not to worry about counting beyond 20. You've landed! So one bag up front, one in back and off we go. Five of the guys are going up to higher altitudes, something like 8,000 feet, but I would getting off at 3 or 5, just high enough to step out, jump, count to 10 and pull the rip cord. Simple enough. On the way up I am next to the open door, last in but first out, and getting hit by strong winds coming off the propeller. To calm my nerves I start singing "Oh my bags are packed, I'm ready to go, sitting here inside the door, can't wait to get out and say good-bye. . ." Slight change from John Denver or Peter, Paul and Mary's version. After sticking my arm out and having it whipped back I mention how hard getting out would be. Novice! They assure me the engine would be turned off before I stepped out. And it was, suddenly there was this total silence, just floating along. . . . but no time to enjoy the moment. Get up, get out. I step quickly onto a foot pad attached to the single wing strut, holding the strut I enjoy a short look down. Wow, bird's eye view of the earth. Time to fly. They say jump, I jump, backward and sort of arched. See, I actually do listen. Then a quick count to 20. . . or was it 10. . . or 5. . . pull the rip cord and bingo, the chute opens. Hallelujah. Second chute not needed. Then the incredible rush accentuated by a few loud shouts. After the tension and adrenaline subside the thrill of doing something for the first time takes over, my body hanging in space. OK, time to locate the landing area. Wow, way over there. . . why? Why not directly below? How to steer this canopy, get that hole in the chute where it belongs? I pull down the left handle and spin left, I pull down the right handle and spin right. Corkscrew left, corkscrew right, still dropping straight down. Below there is a track of homes, all of which are coming up fast. In front of those homes are power lines, telephone, and electric, whatever. Shit! So I start trying to move or guide the flight of this parachute with body English, something not taught in sky school. The houses and power lines are waiting but luckily the chute carries me into some backyard, right into a huge bamboo tree with its shoots pointing straight up like spears. I land right in the very middle of the tree. Bamboo shoots may be good to eat but not great for colonoscopies or prostate exams. Inches in any direction and I would have been human shish kabob. Instead my parachute is hanging over a tree in a residential backyard. Soon a little Hawaiian kid comes crawling through the bamboo, looks up at me and asks, 'what da matta for you bro'? 'You backyard bro, no da kind? 'I ask if he can go get help and he says 'you miss landing plenty, heh? 'Funny! I was hanging in his playground. He leaves and within 10 minutes the rescue team is there wondering what kind of a mess they will be cleaning up? All is good save for the parachute, which would require some stitches. Not I, not one, not a scratch. Lucky Luke rides (flies) again. My first and last attempt at sky diving, well whatever that jump was called... it was a perfect 10, and a perfect example of "a cat's innate ability to orient itself as it falls in order to land on its feet." The only loss was another one of those cute little cat lives inherited at birth.

4 -Lets stick with diving. . . . less sky but more water -

As mentioned I lived in Hawaii for the better part of seven years. This period was a social and physical 'free for all'. . . literally. During those years I either worked or lived on all the islands save for Lanai, Kahoolawe and Niihau. During a visit to Maui I was playing along a sandy shore near the Sheraton Hotel along with some guy with much darker skin. We were both diving into the shore break, frolicking between sand and waves. He spoke to me in broken English, (from Puerto Rico I think) asking if I like to dive? Sure, but I assumed he was referring to snorkeling or skin diving. He asked if I wanted to go dive. Why not? So off we go toward the hotel, climbing up the Maui Sheraton bluffs, the cliffs near the hotel. I then asked what kind of diving he's talking about and he says 'high diving. 'He wants to jump off the bluffs. In those days everything needed to be attempted at least once, but I was not fond of high places. That 10 meter board at public swimming pools was the limit, anything above that would damage my courage meter. At the top he shows me the routine, what to do. Leap out parallel to the water, not down, spread the arms, lift the head, feel the wind and time the jump to an incoming wave. I just now Googled those Sheraton bluffs and the photos offered make that cliff look less threatening. Why did it seem like 15-20 meters back then? Maybe it was not that dangerous for him. Anyway, he tells me to watch and learn then starts with crossing himself like a good Catholic. . . . three times. He looks down, looks out and jumps, arms wide, gracefully sailing into the Pacific. Hardly a splash. My turn. That adrenaline rush returns. Time for some spiritual crossing, three is good. Look down, spread the wings, find a wave, and feel scared and go... out, gravity and splash. Not bad, so up we go for round two. Once again no problem, what a rush. Back up for a third shot of adrenaline. And on that dive I make a slight mistake, bending my hands flat instead of pointing them straight into the water. The back of my hands hit the water, then my head, smacking my chrome dome like a frying pan, turning the lights out for a split second. I went down deep before the cobwebs cleared and was lucky to regain the surface. Three strikes and we were both out. None of these episodes would be life threatening for those who love danger and like to live on the edge. But one man's fun can be another man's folly. Mistakes are usually due to having more foolish confidence than ability. Still, that cat took some nice long dives and always landed wet. . . . but well!

5 – The road railing at Simplon Pass in the Swiss Alps -

This one will get windy as it allows for some digression and a lot of background. It is the perfect chance to share bits of that first trip to Europe and why the trip lasted so long. I came to Europe the first time after I got out of the Coast Guard in Hawaii. I had 8 or 9 hundred dollars in the pocket and only a one way ticket. I landed in Brussels and after one month in Holland, hitched my way up to Copenhagen. Two months had gone by as had most of my money . I wanted to stay in Europe longer and needed a job. While in the states I had driven several one-way u-drive cars across the USA, allowing me to see much of North America without spending a dime and I wondered if such a thing might exist in Europe, in this case Denmark? So I randomly asked some Dane where the nearest car rental agency was, not Hertz or Avis. Those were the two biggies back then. He directed me to some small agency over near the Central Train Station. The agency no longer exists so the name is not important. Anyway I went in and asked if they had any cars they needed delivered in Europe? Instead of a big no, they sent me upstairs to some guy on the second floor sitting at a desk in front of a board with lines and numbers. I asked if he needed someone to deliver cars in Europe... and he asked "where I wanted to go?" I said anywhere and everywhere. He explained that he had over 70 cars that needed to be delivered to different cities around Europe, mainly to AAA members coming over from the USA. Unfu.. ....believable! As it turned out this was the absolute only car rental agency in all of Europe that offered such a program, delivering cars to cities all over Europe without charging their customers any delivery or return fees. Crazy good!

Their free delivery policy had to do with some strange Danish tax law written to encourage car rental agencies to purchase their vehicles in Denmark from Danish dealerships. Then after something like 20,000 kilometers, the state tax for that car was refunded, allowing the agency to sell their slightly used vehicles for nearly what was paid for it new. Something like that. Out of pure luck (serendipity) I end up being directed to this one of a kind agency. So that was the beginning of a year in Copenhagen, Denmark, one of the best cities in Europe.... and one of the best years of my vagabond life. It was also the start of delivering/driving free cars of every make all around the continent, traveling some 100,000 miles to nearly every country on both sides of the Iron Curtain, save for Russia. It was a year of meeting international women, learning bits of 6 languages... and eventually living for short periods with some 60 different families. It was also a year of learning how to sleep in the back seat of rental cars while traveling nearly every road in Central Europe. Upon returning to the USA after a year and a half, I received 53 Christmas cards from those European families and friends I met. I will try to get back to this period later, but now what about Simplon Pass and that railing? Whenever I drove a car to some city like Vienna, Salzburg, Venice, Rome, Lisbon, Paris, Amsterdam, Munich, Brussels, Brugge, Oslo, Stockholm, Zurich, Geneva etc., there were often two cars waiting to bring back to Copenhagen or to deliver elsewhere in Europe. I could only drive one car myself so I would go into youth hostels and ask out loud if anyone wanted to drive a free car to such and such city, usually Copenhagen. The kids at those hostels jumped at the chance, in fact some thought it was too good to believe, that there was probably drugs stashed in the car.

Most wanted to go anyway, a chance to drive their own car rather than hitch hike or take the train. They would have to show me a driver's license and passport and sign a contract, allowing them three or four days delivery time. No rush. What the kids did not know is that the deal should have been even sweeter, that the petrol was also included. I would collect the gas money for each car delivered and that is how I earned just enough to break even driving/delivering rental cars for one year. Sorry, back to the railing. There were two cars in Venice, Opel kadetts that needed to be driven back to Copenhagen. I found a kid from Minnesota at some Venice hostel and off we went. A nice burly young kid who turned out to be a solid driver and big help. It was late autumn and getting colder. I recall trying to find a patch of grass in Venice to sleep on. Pretty rare, but there was one surrounded by a tall spiked fence. I jumped over, laid down the sleeping bag and was out. During the night I kept hearing some crunching sounds beneath the bag and just assumed it was fallen autumn leaves. When I awoke in the morning there were all these little shiny pathways across my bag and realized the source of those crunching sounds. . . . snails. Squished escargot everywhere! Enough side tracks. We drove the two Opel kadetts as far as Switzerland by sunset and hoped to possibly get over Simplon Pass that night. Crossing the Italian/Swiss border we stop at passport control and the policeman pointed to our tires and indicated 'no good'. A kadett back then was built about as strong as a beer can, and about as light. We fail to heed his warning and off into the dusk light we go, heading toward Simplon Pass, 2002 meters up. Dusk turned to night and we kept climbing and winding, one sharp turn after the next, most of which were without guardrails. Mountain walls on one side, nothing but space on the other. It was dark so I just kept following the tail lights from his Opel, turn after turn. Suddenly his taillights took an extra wiggle, then straightened back out. When I started into the same bend I heard what sounded like gravel. It was black ice. . . and off I went, first weaving, then spinning toward the dark space beyond the curve. Not even time for an adrenaline kick, just grip and get ready to fly. The next second the car is being tossed back onto the road still spinning out of control and eventually rolling backward toward that same black abyss. The car bounces again, and stops. I open the door, walk over to the edge and look down into the dark. . . and then the slightly bent railing at my knees. Lucky Luke. Serendipity.

The other guy is a few hundred meters up the road when he notices my headlights are not in his rear view mirror. He turns, comes back down and finds me looking over the railing into the valley below. Both headlights and taillights of my Opel are gone, smashed by the railing. Back then railings were not wrapped around every turn on the many mountain passes that traversed the Swiss Alps. They were the exception, not the rule. I silently thanked the engineer or crew that constructed this one, the one that keep my car from going airborne. There was a small hotel only a couple of kilometers up the road and we managed to drive to it and spent the night. Next morning we still had the audacity/stupidity to take both cars on over the pass and eventually on to Copenhagen, driving by day only.

The cat sacrificed that night did not choose to fly Swiss Air.

6 – The Rocky Mountains of Utah –

I was attending the University of Utah on a one year athletic scholarship, running the mile for their track team. I actually had two close calls on this same mountain and both are worth sharing. It's called Mount Alta. In the old wooden dormitory where I roomed, called Wasatch, named after the Wasatch Mountains, I made friends with a kid from Canada who was the Canadian Junior Ski champion, and who was also on a sports scholarship. We decided to climb the main peak at Alta, to help us both get in better shape, him for skiing, me for running. We made the top on a lovely sunny day and noticed a lake half way down the mountain on our return walk. We decided then to go back in a couple weeks with fishing poles. On that second hike I was dressed in jeans and normal hiking shoes, nothing water resistant or thermal. As we climbed a slight snow started falling and by the time we reached the little lake it was a full on snow storm carried by blinding cold winds. It buried the mountain and us within an hour and soon my fingers and feet were frozen. I was so cold I could hardly move and I sat down to rest. It felt great to just sit there. This Canadian kid grew up in these conditions, while I was braving the endless summers of

Southern California. Luckily he was tough enough for both of us and he pulled me up and started pushing me and would not let me stop. I had cheap leather gloves on that froze to my fingers so he helped me pull them off, after which I stuck both hands inside my pants. He kept me going until we got down the mountain far enough to locate a cabin where we were forced to break down the front door and take shelter. No blankets but there was a mattress which we rolled into like a double burrito. There we stayed for hours until the storm subsided. Once back to the car we got the heater going and I kept rubbing my hands together, trying to get the feeling back, not knowing by so doing I was doing permanent damage, busting tiny blood vessels. Working frostbite out of body parts is tricky and painful. A few of my fingers were frostbitten and never did work right in cold weather after that episode.

Alta tried to stick it to me a second time, and by coincidence it was with that same Canadian, this time while partaking in his favorite sport and profession, skiing. I had never been on skis other than water skis, and maybe a surfboard or two, yet I felt fully capable to try anything. I also let the Canadian convince me skiing would be easy and so we headed to Alta once again, shortly after a snow storm had painted the Utah Rockies and its many ski runs. All slopes were open and all lifts spinning. He took me right to the very top, lift after lift after lift, ever upward. What the hell, anyone can sit in a chair with skis on. I thought I was doing pretty well just to ski between the lifts. It was not long after sunrise and the snow was icy at the top. The perfect surface for beginners and only 10,000 feet high, nearly two miles up. My Canadian buddy guided me over to the start of the highest slope and then says, "Let's go". 'Give me a minute'. . . so he pushes off alone onto that first run which looks endless. . . and straight down! As he goes sailing down the icy slope he starts pirouetting, then sideways, backwards, forwards. . . . more like ice-skating than skiing. When he stops at the bottom he is this tiny little ant, waving at me to go. Another friend drops off the lift and comes over to say, "Ready". 'In a minute! 'Then there are two tiny ants at the bottom, both waving me on. Scared shit less is probably not the way to start your first run but it was either ski down or take all those lifts back to the bottom and later explain why. So I cast off, dropping like running down a ski jump ramp. A straight line at full throttle. Even if I knew how, turning or even sitting was no longer an option. Where the hell were the brakes? To add to the adventure the skis I had on were wooden antiques sporting those old handles with steel cables that went back around the heel pulling the toe into a metal clamp. Not the latest in ski bindings... nor the safest. Half way down my eyes were watering so badly everything is a blur, including my two friends as I flew passed. Goggles might have helped. I was creating a new Olympic ski event; 'The Straight Downhill for idiots'... no turning allowed, no goggles, no practice, no hope! At the bottom of the run a maneuver was required due to rocks and trees but nothing was visible ... or negotiable. All ahead full until my skis hit something and catapulted me into space. My two buddies soon realized who the blur was that just flew past and turned to watch a spectacular lift off. A thing of beauty they later told me. Both found me buried head first in a huge pile of soft snow surround by white lumps..... rocks. Only my feet were sticking out and they grabbed those, one leg each, pulled me out, got me upright and started brushing away the snow, checking body parts. When all limbs were accounted for and I stopped shaking I looked up the slope and noticed a ski stuck into the snow about 20 yards above us, planted straight up. They said when I set sail the ski did likewise, rotating a few times in the air before sticking the landing. They gave both me and the ski a 10. We searched for the second ski and never did find it. One of the guys went up to retrieve the planted ski and what he brought back validated the violence of the crash. The entire length of that wooden ski was split and the front toe clamps were flattened. It seems I went right out the front door when the skis hit something. The Canadian had to put me on the back of his skis and help slide me down to the next lift below. That first day of skiing ended as it began, sitting on a chair.

While I enjoyed the style points awarded, it was one and done. I did not ski again for 25 years, until I moved to Sweden. I was feeling lucky to be leaving Alta for the last time with all body parts still connected. Two cats, one nearly frozen and the other nearly dismantled, but as it was all on the same mountain, it only gets counted as one.

7 – Fishing on The Yakima River in Washington -

This would be the only fishing vacation ever taken with my Mom and her second husband, my step-dad, Bob. We went camping up in Washington on the Yakama River in the early summer. The river was carrying tons of snow melt, gushing down the valley like a long broken string of white water. That first morning I am up and out early, but after an hour I have yet to find any section of the river calm enough to lay a line in. Then I notice a huge beaver dam connecting both banks of the river and strong enough to walk on. I make it to the other side foolishly following that old adage, 'the grass is always greener on the other side.' After crossing I continue working my way up river looking for a calm spot. Morning turns into afternoon and the going gets tougher. The dirt road that parallels the river is on the other side. . . of course. The vegetation near the river becomes too thick to plow through so I am forced to go higher up into the tree line, then every hundred yards or so I drop back down to check the river. Nothing, no breaks and the day is getting shorter, probably already too late to go back the way I came. Not to panic, I can always stay the night and make it back tomorrow. . . but do not relish the thought. Next trip down to the river presents a possible opportunity. There is a big pine tree half in the water and half onshore, reaching out about a fourth of the way across the river, pointing downward. I hug the log with both arms and legs and start to shimmy down, holding my fishing rod in one hand. The plan was to hang on, slide to the end of the log, let go and hope to dog paddle the rest of the way the across the Yakama with pole in hand. As I near the end of the log I feel the grip of the current and realize this is sure suicide. With a few feet left I roll back over the log to the side blocked from the current and claw my way back up to the shore. It's not worth it. I am not a strong swimmer and in such cold torrent waters with shoes, chances of making it across would be slim to none. A night in the forest was the safer choice. So back up the mountain I go to the tree line. Instead of retracing my tracks downriver I try one more bend and then back down to the riverbank. "I don't believe what I'm seeing". There lies a giant fallen fir tree across the whole river, 80 feet of trunk connecting both banks. That line from the Simon and Garfunkel song, "Bridge Over Troubled Water."

I climb up, walk the log over, find the road, breathe easy and get back to thinking fish knowing camp is just a walk or hitch hike away. Eventually a calm pool in the river shows itself loaded with hundreds of trout. Out comes the legal limit within minutes and once on the road a car comes by and delivers me and the fish back to camp before dusk. Nothing better than freshly caught fish pan fried. Cats love it!

8 – Another car crash – California Hwy. 299 from Arcata to Redding -

This is a pretty dangerous winding road out of Arcata and one afternoon a girlfriend of mine from Humboldt State College asked if I would like to go for a ride in her new 1961 Austin Healy, probably a present from her parents. Why not, pretty girl, nice wheels. She heads East on Hwy. 299 out of Arcata, a highway with blind curves, cliffs and demonic logging trucks. Up to Willow Creek it is mostly hairpin turns and not a road to take lightly. The Austin Healy was a convertible, and had some pep in its engine. She went up the winding road for some miles and then about dark turned her sports car around and headed back, mostly down grades. All was good, but like riding a horse, going up is always safer or easier than going down. For some crazy reason she felt the urge to show off her new toy and hit the throttle going into a sharp turn. The car was going way too fast to make the inside turn, where the mountain was. She hit the rocky side of the hill out of control and luckily the wall knocked the car back onto four wheels and helped guide us around the bend, sparks flying past my window from the front wheel base and door. It was like sitting on a spot welding assembly line. The Healy stayed upright, though the driver was no longer in control. The mountain wall on the bend carried us around the curve upright, but then the sports car continued across the road and over the mountain edge, the side that drops off. We did drop, but only a few feet into a big ditch waiting just below the road. You might say we were caught in a rut, or by a rut. There is an old saying that 'the only difference between a rut and the grave is the depth, 'especially true in this case. My girlfriend had head butted the windshield, but luckily did not fly through. She was knocked out but still in the car. We sat in that ditch until she shook out the cobwebs and started to talk. There was something warm running down her face and it wasn't tears. Our only exit was out my door and it took a while. Once up, we actually felt giddy, laughing, and happy to be alive. Her scalp wound needed stitches, but it was minor damage considering what could have been. She was taken to some hospital, the car to some repair shop, and me to my trailer park below the college campus, a metal box called home in which I later lost my virginity. Driving accidents can waste a lot of cat lives.

9 – Africa – So many close calls, so many memories -

I love Africa, in fact nothing leaves deeper impressions than the sunsets, wildlife and sensory impressions collected there. The following draws from a couple of those special moments.

During our 19 month journey around the world, Donna and I made it to Nairobi, Kenya and there at the Stanley Hotel stood a famous communication center, an old thorn tree that was once used as a public message board. The Thorn Tree Cafe at the Stanley Hotel was named in memory of that original tree. A thousand pieces of paper were always pinned to its big trunk and on one of those papers was a note from a couple seeking travelers to share expenses for a safari through Tanzania. The couple had been running tour groups and safaris around that part of Africa for over 7 years, mostly in Kenya, Tanzania, Mozambique and Zimbabwe. The couple was a lady from Australia and a guy from England and they wanted one last run into Tanzania before packing it in and going back to their home lands. Along with the two of us, three Germans signed on and so it was lucky number 7 setting off in their trusty, rusty old land rover. Lucky for us, this duo knew all the tricks of the trade when it came to border crossings and national park managers. It required all their ingenuity and experience to get us through. The border was closed at that time due to yet another war between Kenya and Tanzania. They knew tires and fuel would be scarce once out of Kenya so they loaded up several jerry cans of gasoline and four additional off road tires. Once at the border the games began between our guides and the guards. Our resourceful duo employed a cross between bribery and ransom. How much money, which currency, how many cigarettes, and how much gas would it take to get us into Tanzania? The game took hours and required a lot of bluffing and patience but two jerry cans and a carton of cigarettes later we were over the border driving the rough road to Arusha, hoping to get there before dark due to the packs of bandits that patrolled Northern Tanzania. The road was so rough it tore up four tires and by dusk we were down to the final four, and one of those was slowly coming apart. We stopped a couple of time to cut off a strip of rubber from the tire that was hitting its wheel well. Our magnificent seven limped into Arusha and parked the land rover at one of the auto repair shops for the night. Next day we asked the owner of the shop how long it would take to get a couple of spare tires and he said, "ohh, about a year, maybe two!" Not good! Even our guide's ingenuity was not going to solve this mess. If we were going to be in Tanzania for a year I might as well make some new friends so I walk over and start a conversation with some complete stranger having his car repaired inside the shop. That hello resulted in another crazy case of serendipity at its finest. This guy was the brother of the only person in all of Tanzania I actually knew, a man I had been communicating with by mail over the past year. His brother was the national park authority for Mount Kilimanjaro and a friend of a friend in Sweden. I had been writing to this guy's brother before we left for Kenya, trying to work out two visitor's passes and the chance to climb Kilimanjaro as part of our travels in Africa. As it turned out this park manager wanted/demanded so many gifts (bribery) for his favorable treatment that I eventually let it slide. Weather conditions during our time in Kenya and now Tanzania were so cloudy that Kilimanjaro was hidden the whole time anyway. But here I am talking to some stranger who just happens to be the brother of "my dear friend and pen pal from Mount Kilimanjaro", (a person I admire and am longing to meet. Ha ha) It turns out their whole family was politically connected with some serious clout. The next thing we know this guy I am talking to is giving orders to the shop owner, telling him to jack up some other land rover and give us the tires. We get two, maybe three tires from another rover and are soon on our way. What just happened? I almost broke this guy's hand shaking it while telling him to be sure and pass along my warm regards to his wonderful brother, and how much I was going to miss seeing that great mountain. . . and for him to be sure to visit me should he ever come over to Southern California. I'm still waiting.

Next stop is the bank. Back then you were required to exchange a minimum amount of Western currency per day per person. So the Aussie goes in to one of the few banks in Arusha and exchanges about $20. Then she brings the form back to the rover and adds a zero to the $20 and off we go. Next stop is Lake Manyara National Park. Beautiful! Then over to Ngorongoro Crater and that first little adventure. The jewel in Ngorongoro's crown is a deep, volcanic crater. But first how to avoid paying the big fees, or bribes at the park entrance? The park manager questions our paperwork from the bank. Very astute! He says it looks phony and so the standoff begins. Instead of backing down and paying the fees the English bloke calls him out, telling the manager to call the bank in Arusha and ask. . . and if he did not let us into the park we would be calling the Ministry of Tourism in Arusha to report his actions. The Britt knew there wasn't a telephone within fifty miles, neither was there any Ministry of Tourism. We end up giving the park attendant some bars of soap (in great demand) in exchange for a park pass, then get assigned one of his prize park guides. The guide is stoned, but before he falls asleep he gets into that preferred shotgun seat, the one us photographers fight for. Once into Ngorongora we kick down a dusty road keeping pace with an ostrich that seems to be racing us. The guide wakes up, looks out his wasted window and claims, 'that is a male ostrich'. Then falls back into his coma. It was the last we heard from him. That afternoon we park next to a huge thorn tree in the crater and set up our little camp. Being in this vast crater seemed rather safe so Donna and I place our tent about 50 feet from the land rover with a nice panoramic view. Then we all pile back into the rover for a sunset cruise, which included two male black rhinos, a cheetah, more ostrich, warthogs, and a couple of lions. Back at camp before dinner Donna and I walk over to a nearby group of tents about 100 yards away. Sitting in the camp is a black guy with a gun. I ask why the gun? He says a couple of lions came in and tore up one of their tents the night before. We walk back to our minicamp and quickly relocate our tent, placing it right next the land rover, almost tying it off to a tire and directly under a huge thorn tree. Safety in numbers. Night comes and into our 5 star polyester hotel Donna and I go, me with my trusty tripod. I always thought of my camera tripod as a first and last defense. I never did pack a gun or even a hunting knife. Hard to enter airplanes or cross borders with those items. During the early part of the night a lot of snorting comes walking in, a big family of warthogs. They start sniffing along the tent right near our heads and we wonder when they will invite themselves in? It's only a synthetic wall and these pigs are packing the perfect openers, two on either side of their ugly long snouts. Hundreds of pounds of potentially mean bacon is snorting in our ears while I sit there nearly naked with my tripod. We are both frozen in fear. The tension mounts and I finally yell at the Aussie and Brit, who are sleeping safely on the roof of their land rover, to climb down and chase the bloody pigs away. He yells back, "not to worry. . . go to sleep." "If it's a lion wake me and I'll try to take some souvenir shots (photos, not bullets)." So after about 30 minutes the warthogs depart. Sleep at last!

Hours later in the middle of the night there is some serious noise from above, crunching and ripping sounds. It's an elephant taking branches off the thorn tree overhead (how they can chew those big thorns is a mystery). This elephant is making the earth vibrate, straddling our tent while eating dinner. One misstep could produce human pancakes. Sleeping in a tent under an elephant is nerve racking. You don't breathe, you don't yell and you certainly don't climb out with a tripod.

You get religious. An hour of breaking, crunching and earth moving before silence returns. Not much sleep later sunrise slowly starts washing away the darkness, light crawling across the crater floor, erasing the night. . . and the tension. Donna hears me moaning about the sleepless night, first the warthogs and then the bloody elephant. "WHAT ELEPHANT?"

'You must be kidding, you did not hear the elephant?'

'BS, she says?' I tell her it was standing right over us for an hour. 'BS!' I open the tent flap and in the dirt a few inches away is a collection of footprints, the largest any animal can make on this planet. She looks down at the dirt and gasps. I ask if these prints are from her feet? (Maybe. . . . if her feet were as big as her boobs!)

On to Serengeti National Park. On the way we stop at a luxury hotel hoping for a beer and some food. The country is at war and tourists are not to be found. Neither is food or drink. The hotel is empty, including the kitchen, the swimming pool and most of the toilets. They offer us one egg. . . any style. We eat our egg and leave. Border wars with five star hotels going to waste. We actually spent over a week in Tanzania, five days crossing the Serengeti and did not see another tourist. Hallelujah. Once in a lifetime. During the trip, I believe it was at Lake Manyara, we had another moment. It was late afternoon and the three Germans were riding on the roof of the rover while the four of us were inside. A park ranger came by and reported the sighting of a rhino in the area. Soon after we saw it go into some thick brush that was taller than the land rover. We approached the bush and one of the Germans from above says the rhino is only a few feet away, standing just out of sight. The rhino heard the motor and charged full speed out of bush leaving the Britt no time to turn. He jams the rover into reverse and floors it. The rhino is only about 10 yards away, the four of us looking out the front window as he charges. Reverse gear for a land rover is not that fast and the Britt could not see where he is going. The rover hits a rock and two of the Germans go flying over the side but each catch the roof rack railing on the way over and hang on, legs pumping while the land rover is reversing itself away from the rhino. It lasts only a few seconds, but the visual images will live forever. The rhino stops and the Germans remount the roof. Not a single photograph to record the moment. Sometimes the cat is just too busy saving itself.

But now we are in the Serengeti. . . alone with all the wildlife but low on food and fuel. Our last night was magical. Nothing left in the food locker save for a package of spaghetti and tobasco sauce. . . . and two bottles of wine. Perfect. The tobasco sauce made the spaghetti nearly impossible to eat so it became a liquid last supper. Our tent was on one side of this little campsite with its wooden table and the rover and Germans on the other. That night a family of baboons came in and found the two empty bottles

and started tapping the table with them. The bottles were never broken and after about an hour they went away. Maybe that is because the next visitor fed on baboons and just about every other member of the animal kingdom. It was a lion, walking around with a low growl. It never did come up to the tent, but was near or in camp. In the morning I shall never forget seeing that plate of spaghetti with the tobasco. . . . still uneaten! That was some seriously bad cuisine. Neither lion nor baboon touched it. But what Donna and I woke up to was like a dream, a National Geographic production. From our open tent we could see thousands of wildebeest walking through the valley floor below. Then a train of zebras walked down the slope a hundred yards away, followed by a train of giraffes. We got out and went over to a rock to watch, away from our campsite. After an hour we recalled the lion in our camp and realized they follow these migrations and had to be in the area. No sense adding to a lion's menu. If they only knew how defenseless and tasty humans were. No thick skins, no scales, no feathers, no claws, no dangerous tusks or canines, and slow afoot. Just soft tender meat on the bone.

Imagine if animals could take away our guns? A level playing field between humans and wildlife. A more honest form of combat. Let the games begin.

Fan duel or DraftKings and all the other betting systems could expand beyond today's sporting world to include animals, say a wolverine against a man (well trained man) in the octagon. How about a wolf vs. man, straight up, no weapons. Mmmmmmmm. A big martial arts professional vs. a hippo or water buffalo? You could lay odds on a goose or swan against a semi fit female. Endless possibilities. . . and real blood. No guns, no more homicides. You could take a small portion of the 9000 lives saved annually from the elimination of firearms and toss them into octagons. Real MMA matches, "Man vs. Mammal". Raw action! Toss a python or crock in the ring vs. some drug dealer or rapist, maybe a person caught for human trafficking vs. a pit bull or wolverine, panther, gorilla, or male baboon. A prize male lion vs. the big game hunter without his high powered rifle. What about that dentist, Walter, who shot Cecil the lion in Zimbabwe. Walter vs. Cecil in the octagon. Pay per view! People would eat it up, well maybe literally if the loser could be served on some menu after the fight. . . like in "Fried Green Tomatoes." The possibilities are endless. A panther or a bear vs. Bernie Madoff or some Wall Street con artist. . . maybe just a skunk against a kid! I mean thousands of kids are gunned down aimlessly anyway. Scratches and stinky clothing are better and more entertaining than homicides. If we get tired of octagon battles we could put humans, especially the Taiwanese, into huge aquariums with sharks, sharks that still had their dorsal fins. Who wouldn't pay big money for that action? Hell, make it fair and toss in a Taiwanese tag team with swim fins against a single great white.

OK, I'm zoning out. Again.

Back to the cat lives, mine. Well not before putting the Tabby cat I once owned named Bambino into the octagon with an X neighbor.

Just like the movie, "Out of Africa". . . memoirs take detours.

I knew a few families in Zimbabwe that owned tobacco plantations. One family had their own airplane and during a visit they took me with them on vacation to Tiger Bay Resort on Lake Kariba. We flew across Zimbabwe in their plane. They also owned a houseboat which was became our hotel on the lake and attached was a motor boat which could be used for water skiing. The tricky part about water skiing on Lake Kariba is that it is encircled by a huge crocodiles, and some of these large aquatic reptiles had learned that houseboats tossed food overboard, so tailgating for garbage was becoming an issue. Crocks were trolling the lake like scavengers. This tended to make water skiing a bit more challenging, and foolish. The foolish part was falling, especially if near any shoreline. The idea was to stay upright, then release the tow line as near to the houseboat as possible without crashing into it. It added a new dimension to water skiing unlike what we experienced back in Hawaii.

Fortunately the only crock that got near me on that trip happened while photographing one evening. That sunset the clouds over the lake were painted in crimson and I was painted in gin tonics. I did not see the scaly submarine with its tiny twin periscopes slowly approaching in the waning light. This giant was only a few yards away when the red skies reflected off its peepers. Two of us saw it at the same time and I grabbed my tripod and we both exited the shore. Later that night I set my tripod and camera out near the houseboat to record some star trails. After an hour there was some snorting going on near the boat and our floodlight traced a large herd of water buffalo circling my camera. That is where it stayed for the night.

By morning that photo was slightly over exposed.

Where does that dead cat come into this story? Take your pick. . . but the choice has to include the flight back across Zimbabwe. Shawna was a pilot as was her husband Keith, and one had to get back home to the tobacco farm. That part is foggy. What I do remember is that the flight was pretty long, a couple of hours across a good portion of Zimbabwe. The fuel tanks are in the wings and both gauges on the control panel plainly indicated the tanks were getting closer to empty. I asked if she could land the plane in the bush and she wasn't sure, she had never tried. We kept flying and the two needles kept dropping until both were bobbing on the empty line, then stopped bobbing. We landed on their plantation and taxied to the hanger, both of us looking relieved and laughing. Shawna took out a wooden stick and checked the tanks. The stick echoed off the bottom of each wing, a hallow metal sound. Flying on fumes is exciting if you live to tell about it. That cat landed thirsty.

It's hard to leave Zimbabwe without mentioning what a beautiful special and fairly safe country it was back in the 80's. I just Googled the name Mugabe, one of the most evil men on this planet, a corrupt despot that NATO and the Western World has turned a blind eye to. He took a perfectly lovely country and destroyed it, turning the one source of economic stability and productivity into the enemy, the white tobacco farmer. White people settled Rhodesia as far back as blacks did, many generations ago. They fought the war against Zambia, blacks and whites together. Then came Mugabe in 1991. He turned blacks against whites, convincing blacks that white people had stolen their lands. The tobacco farms that provided the number one export and source of social and financial stability, were confiscated and within months turned back into dirt. Whites were terrorized, beaten and forced to leave or suffer the consequences, jail or death. You might watch the new documentary that just came out called, 'Mugabe and the White African,' charting one family's extraordinary courage in the face of state sanctioned terror. Once again another beautiful country destroyed by an evil leader. Actually thought I would retire in another such country, Argentina. I got married there, bought a beautiful house there, planned to photograph and play golf there, drink fine Mendoza wine and gracefully grow old there Argentine style.

Then another of those looney leaders came into power, Nestor Kirchner, the husband of the next president, Cristina Ferandez de Kirchner. These two nut cases controlled the country since 2003 and pretty much ruined everything that was once good and decent about it, save for the vast natural beauty. There is so much crime on the streets of Buenos Aires that few tourists still want to visit. The country is broke, currency is devalued monthly, banks don't function and the city streets are lawless. Argentine people have turned to bartering, not buying. The country desperately needs new blood, as does Zimbabwe. Countries with lousy leaders have also made tourist travel much less desirable.

This is getting off the memoir trail but it is sad and insane how so many great countries of the world are ruined by poor leadership. Once in control of the police and military, rivals are eliminated as is the free press. Its game, set, match. At the time of this writing Argentina had finally found a new leader so perhaps the Kirchner crimes will soon be history.

Before following the movie "Out of Africa" it would be nice to share a few other special moments. It may not seem life threatening but after seeing a travel program the other night taken from the Zambezi River in Zimbabwe I felt compelled to add the following. This documentary TV special I watched had some guy going along in a large motor boat with his filming crew, pointing out hippos on the move from a great distance, saying how dangerous they were, warning the viewer to be ready for anything. Deep river, big boat and 50 yards to the nearest hippo, all the while expounding on the dangers.

My turn. I wish I had been in the business of doing adventure travel documentaries back in the day. On this particular trip to Zimbabwe I went to Lake Kariba to meet up with some guide that was to help me capture a few wildlife photos. I recall he was a rugby player who actually played on the National Zimbabwe side. Besides working on the family farm he was a guide for big game hunters. He agreed to a bit of hunting using my favorite weapon, an old Nikon with a 200mm lens. So we met up at Lake Kariba on his family's houseboat and the next morning set off in a tiny outboard motor not much longer than a dingy, big for an aluminum bathtub, small for a boat. Huge Nile Crocodiles inhabit the lake as do many hippos and we were looking for both on something like a pregnant tin can with a motor. Eventually we came to a huge pod of water lilies and he plowed a path through, pushing the pods aside with an oar, heading for an inlet that he knew was populated with the aforementioned. The little bay was not very deep and was encircled with reptiles resembling to huge crocodile necklace, sunning themselves like four legged logs and in the middle of the pond was a large family of hippos, all staring at us. My guide must have had rugby balls for cojones as he kept motoring right along. Luckily each hippo submerged just as our tiny "African Queen" got near and like submarines with nostrils, bubbles floated to the surface as we passed. Slowly sinking hippos marked by slowly rising bubbles encompassed our aluminum bath tub. We could not have been more than 3-5 feet above each hippo, in fact the guide kept raising the motor as we slid over to prevent the prop from taking a bite. That would have been a dead cat for sure. Through and over the hippos he went like some Disneyland ride.

Pure nuts. . . . more his than mine! Soon the hippo family in the pond was joined by half the crock population sliding in one at a time slowly filling this big muddy swimming pool. It was a popular inlet and we were now the main attraction. Come on in, the water's fine. . . . and rising! Had we crashed the wrong party? He went straight across the inlet to the opposite side until we got stuck in the muddy shallows. Our tin can came to a halt, literally stuck in the mud. And then the motor quit. This after annoying all the locals. By now the family of hippos and flotilla of crocks had us written on their lunch menus. A small filter in the motor was clogged with silt. Luckily the guide had dealt with this issue before. He reached under the boat (dark, shallow and scary) and pulled up the motor. He then casually pulled out the tiny filter with calm steady fingers and blew out the silt. A surgeon's hands attached to a rugby body. Perfect! He puts the filter back into place, lowers the motor into the shallow brown water and pulls the cord. . . it starts on the second try. He then slowly backs us out keeping the prop at an angle above the muddy bottom. The hippos have resurfaced but still offer little to photograph other than eyes. Unless a hippo yawns showing those huge lower tusks, they are not very photogenic. These hippos might be annoyed, but not with each other. . . which is what a photographer wants, a good fight, one that does not involve the photographer. Anyway time for our 10 foot African Queen to make its way back across the hippo pond. Round two and all eyes are upon us as we plow a fresh pathway back across the inlet. Once again these not so gentle giants (no animal in Africa kills more people than hippos) give way as we slide over them, bubbles coming up so close you could reach out and touch them, which I did. Once again we pass over these fat subs as he raises the motor to avoid making hippo sushi. It's one thing to have a motor stopped by mud, another by a 2000 pound hippopotamus. That episode was a collection of moments you just enjoy surviving. When we got back to the houseboat he asked if I had taken any good shots? I told him yes, all perfectly exposed on my mind. He said I needed to put something on film and pointed to a lone bull elephant not far from the houseboat. He suggested he could get the elephant to charge him while I took a few shots. I asked if he had any life insurance? He assured me he knew what he was doing and off the houseboat he went walking toward the elephant. The big bull came down the hill to meet this crazy dude, ears out, trunk up, feet stomping the grassy turf. No dust, so once again no dramatic images, but something most will see less than once in a lifetime.

He stopped but the elephant kept coming. The bull then faked a quick charge, raised its trunk, flapped both big ears and stopped. The shot I got shows this guy with his hands crossed over his family jewels (rugby balls), facing a massive bull 10 yards away. After a short stand off the guide turned and casually walked back to the houseboat. He asked if I got anything? I said, 'I got nervous'. . . and another perfectly exposed memory. The photos never sold so the moment will likely only be seen here with words. The other night, some 30 years later, I wondered what this film maker and his crew doing the 'wildlife documentary on the

Zambezi River'would have said and felt had they been with us that day in our pregnant bathtub on Lake Kariba?

Imprints left by Africa go deeper and last longer than those made elsewhere. Before leaving I would like to share a couple more. There was the bungee jump from the Victoria Falls Bridge. One could not ask for a more spectacular setting than from the bridge that separates

Zimbabwe from Zambia. This is arguably the best bungee jump in the world, with a 111 meter dive towards the Zambezi River. Not being that fond of heights, or that brave, I tried to talk the jumping instructor into taking my camera and doing the dive for me. It was late in the afternoon so he promised he would do it the next day. The next day came and I went back to the bridge only to be told the guy was suffering from a bad back and would not be jumping. There was only one sucker left. So I attached a motor drive to my Nikon with fish-eye lens and then someone attached the camera to my right hand with tape. . . while someone else attached other things like cords and harnesses to my legs and body. Once everything was on and buttoned up I stepped out onto a platform far above the Zambezi waters, took a long look down. . . . and jumped. Almost like that sky diving in Hawaii. A pure adrenaline rush. The motor drive started firing soon after taking flight and kept on clicking through 36 frames, while walls, ski and water circled around me. After the long cord stretched itself toward the river, it suddenly stops and flings you back up toward the bridge. You are now hanging upside down bouncing like a yo-yo until some assistant lowers himself on another line, grabs hold and turns you upright, then helps guide you back up to the bridge. The photos I took show some nice veins sticking out of my bald head blended with blurred walls, 36 of the worst shots ever taken by that Nikon. The guy in charge mentions I should go buy the video. Souvenirs are not my thing I tell him, but he says I did a perfect 360 on the way down, something seldom seen. I doubt what he claims so over to the tourist shop I go for a look. Sure enough, the video confirms someone looking like me doing a one full revolution on the way down. . . . likely caused by the weight of the camera. It proved to be my favorite souvenir video for years. . . . until I accidentally recorded over it one day in Stockholm. Bummer. How is wish I had it now to prove to my 17 year old daughter that there was a life before her . . . and the dogs I sleep with. In fact this whole effort is partly to confirm that we do have lives before . . .and maybe after. . . parenthood. But nothing beats visual confirmation. As they say, a picture can be worth a thousand words. Luckily I also have plenty of pictures. But no videos! You just have to Google: Chad Ehlers and then go to the Alamy site. . .

As with all of these cat lives, there are no photographs, just perfectly exposed memories.

SLEEPING WITH THE DOGS –
IV – SERENDIPITOUS JOURNEY

It has been a while since I last visited this project, a book about my own life. . . . . . A life recently relocated to the quiet coastal community of Dana Point just down the road from the previous residence in Laguna Niguel. The house got smaller as did the number of dogs. It's down to three as the best of breed, the mother passed away from skin cancer, something that might be contagious. The dermatologist keeps digging new holes into my own weathered hide discovering things with names like basal and squamous, making parts of my face into human sushi, souvenirs from all that sun on all those beaches around the world, especially the seven years in Hawaii on bikini patrol. I need to get with this personal project before there are no more dogs left to sleep with, there is still some original skin left on my face and what's left is still above ground.

Where has this highway hobo been? How many countries?

I am curious myself.

1- All 50 states in the USA.

2-Andorra	3-Austria	4-Belgium
5-Bosnia	6-Bulgaria	7- Croatia
8-Czech Republic	9-Denmark	10-Estonia
11-Finland	12-France	13-Germany
14-Greece	15-Hungary	16-Iceland
17-Ireland	18-Italy	19-Latvia

20-Liechtenstein	22-Luxembourg	23-Monaco
24-Netherlands	25-Norway	26-Poland
27-Portugal	28-Romania	29-San Marino
30-Slovakia	31-Serbia	32-Spain
33-Sweden1	34-Switzerland	35-United Kingdom
36-Egypt	37-Kenya	38-Seychelles
39-South Africa	40-Tanzania	41-Zambia
42-Zimbabwe	43-Japan	44-Maldives
45-Nepal	46-Indonesia	47-Singapore
48- South Korea	49-China	50-Taiwan
51-Thailand	52-Myanmar(Burma)	53-Australia
54-Tasmania	55-New Zealand	56-Fiji
57-Tonga	58-Cook Islands	59-French Polynesia
60-Argentina	61-Brazil	62-Chile
63-Venezuela	64-Uruguay	65-Costa Rica
66-Saint Lucia	67-Saint Vincent	68-Bahamas
69-Barbados	70-Jamaica and	71-Canada

How a guy who grew up fairly broke without any real profession got to visit so many pieces of the global puzzle is the substance of serendipity and of these memoirs. Some of the following is drawn from different dairies that provided temporary much needed company along the way. Yet most of these travels will be drawn from that not so trustworthy memory bank, those foggy nearly forgotten moments that sleep on the back roads of the mind aging like fine wine, going sour. . . or just evaporating.

In 1970 I had received a much needed gift, an early exit from the Coast Guard due to a medical issue called scoliosis. It saved me from going on holiday to a war torn Vietnam and gave me three years of unexpected freedom and the perfect excuse to say Aloha to our 50th state and hello to all those undiscovered countries waiting the other side of the Atlantic.

I had saved up $800 large, enough to hopefully subsidize 3 months of hitch hiking around as many parts of Europe as possible. There were still a few of those old blank Coast Guard orders, the same ones previously utilized to fly around the states on Air National Guard cargo planes between California, New York, the Mardi Gras in New Orleans, back to California and on to Hawaii. So I filled out a couple more, one to get out of Hawaii at half fare on a commercial flight to California, and then one more from Van Nuys Air National Guard Base to Boston. I was pushing my luck, having not been flagged the first few flights around the states. I filled out one last bogus order, dawned my white Coast Guard uni and set off to visit a girlfriend in Boston. It worked. From Boston the cheapest way to Europe back then was Air Icelandic via Iceland to Brussels.

I knew not a single soul in Europe save for some old lady living part time in Munich and part time on the shores of Waikiki. This was going to be something new and fresh. Back in 1970 $800 was a decent chunk of change. It was time to spread the wealth.

After some interesting moments in Brussels and befriending an American who I traveled to Brugge and Ghent with, I hitched up to Amsterdam and arrived during the World Cup. The Dutch side was playing some one, Germany I think, leaving the streets of Amsterdam void of people, a ghost town. You could have fired a cannon down a city street and not hit a soul. Every pub was packed with loud intoxicated noisy fans, mostly Dutch. One cheerful arm waving guy befriended me and offered me a space in his small attic apartment and life in Europe began. A free bed for a couple weeks which allowed me to dump the large green Kilty backpack somewhere safe and dawn a smaller shoulder bag for easier hitch hiking around the Netherlands. I set sail in every direction, from Amsterdam up to Alkmaar in the north, down to The Hague, Rotterdam and Eindhoven. I finally met a young dark haired Dutch beauty in the small southern village of Dongen near Breda. Her parents lived above and owned a quaint family candy / ice cream shop. Two days of double dipping, a genuine Dutch treat. She had to sneak me in the back door up the staircase to her room after Pop settled in, then an early exit with plenty of vanilla wafers to help sweeten the dawn departure back to Amsterdam. If you look at a map of the Netherlands you will notice the size of the roads around Dongen, places few hitch hikers would discover. The smaller the road the better the feeling. There is always a bus or car to nowhere or somewhere.

After two very inexpensive weeks it was time to hitch further north toward Denmark. The border crossing was at a piece of northern Germany called Flensburg. Evening came and a long line of trucks was strung along the main road on both sides of the border for the night. I headed up a hill to some private residence, jumped the back fence and was standing next to a swimming pool in the dark. The pool storage room offered lounge chairs and a perfect bed for the night. When I awoke there was a six pack of Tuborg next to the chair. To this day I'll never know how it got there but it was not there when I left. Just a small thank you note. The six pack and I headed back to the highway where one of the beers helped me catch the next ride north. One hitch later I was lying next to another main road, this one outside a town called Kolding, snoozing under the midday sun with Copenhagen written on a piece of cardboard propped up against my backpack. A truck driver woke me and asked if I needed a lift. He had a big truck cab, his home on wheels, and offered me a place to sleep that night, the first in Copenhagen. The trucker was from Bern, Switzerland, a family man who became a good friend living right in the middle of Europe. In fact I eventually smuggled a large piece of cut crystal out of Czechoslovakia for his family as a Christmas present. So it started in Europe, one person, one day, one unexpected event, one positive experience at a time. Travelers can become like good will ambassadors and the US needed a few. That truck driver and his family in Bern became the second of some 60 different families that I would eventually spend at least one night with during that year of traveling throughout Europe, friendships that lasted for years and all of which were random and spontaneous. . . . or serendipitous. Being able to travel for so long, to so many places, stay with so many families, starting with only $800. . . .

After the truck cab it was a youth hostel. Also a couple of visits to the Tuborg and Carlsberg factories for their free beer and hot dogs. One sunny day near the center of Copenhagen I stopped a guy at random and asked if he knew of any car rental agency, anything other than Avis or Hertz? He mentioned one next to the central train station, called

Autorist, a two story brick building across from the station. I entered having become familiar with what in the states was called "One Way U-Drive Cars," vehicles that needed delivery to private owners all over the USA. Private parities often had two or three cars only one of which they could drive from their old residence to their new one. These vehicles are left with companies who need drivers, at no cost to the driver. In fact the cars were not only free, gas was included and upon delivery you usually received a nice tip from the owner. I crossed the states a few times this way, taking cars from California to the East Coast, once in a 35 foot RV from Los Angeles to New Hampshire. That story is worth mentioning and it will be the first of many digressions. A little backtracking.

At that time I was living in Torrance and one of my best friends', John Gable, had a Mom, Joyce, who treated me like a son. She had not been East of Nevada and so I drove that huge hotel on wheels to her house and parked out front. The RV stretched from drive way to drive way at her track home. I then went in to ask her if she would like to join me for a drive across the USA that we could visit a good friend we both knew who was attending Harvard University, a surfer and future politician from Hawaii named Leigh Wai Doo. She said it sounded like a wonderful idea but of course she had other things to do at home. I asked her to look out her kitchen window at the street to see what we would be traveling in. She looked, stared the huge RV two minutes, and then started packing. Before leaving we painted a 20 foot poster "From Hawaii to Europe Express" and taped it to the side of our long home on wheels. . . then set off on a 3000 mile luxury tour of middle America. We stopped at every college along the way and invited students in to visit what was for them the biggest RV they had ever seen. For me it was an introduction to new parts of the Midwest and Eastern Seaboard and for Joyce Gable, a chance to visit Leigh Wai in Boston, see something East of Arizona, and then take a train ride back home to Southern California.

Being familiar with this kind of free access to the USA, I entered the rental car agency in Copenhagen and asked if they had any cars they wanted delivered somewhere in Europe. Instead of laughing they told me to go upstairs. There sat a young man at a desk with a lot of numbers connecting lines across the wall behind him. It turned out that all those numbers and lines were cars, cars needing delivery to AAA members coming over from the USA. I asked if he had anything he needed to be delivered in Europe and he asked where I wanted to go. Unf king believable. The Sound of Music.

Anywhere and everywhere I said. It was the beginning of a wonderful yearlong marriage, an opportunity allowing me over 100,000 miles of free travel to nearly every European country. . . . and it was the absolute only car rental agency in all of Europe that offered free deliveries to most every major city. This oddity was made possible by some strange tax arrangement between the Danish government and their car rental agencies. If a Danish agency bought its cars in Denmark and then put 20,000 kilometers on it, the state tax was refunded and the used car could be resold at nearly the original purchase price, or some such weird deal. By pure blind luck I received a free pass to all of Europe. Never be embarrassed to ask questions. That stranger in Copenhagen changed my life forever. Serendipity.

Within days I was living with a lovely Danish girl named Bente in the quiet suburb village of Hellerup. That relationship lasted nearly a year and for three weeks of every month I would be out driving across Europe delivering rental cars to AAA members arriving from the states. Oftentimes there were cars to pick up in a city like Vienna or Rome that needed to be driven to another city like Amsterdam or Paris. Most cars left out in the field needed to be driven back to Copenhagen. It was the chance to see nearly every road in every country and after a couple of weeks of sleeping in various back seats from VWs to Mercedes I would give myself the occasional bath and bunk in some youth hostel. Every month I would go back to Hellerup outside Copenhagen and sleep with my beautiful landlady for a week with bottles of wine from France, Italy or Germany or with one of my three favorite liquors . . . Grand Marnier, Drambuie or Cointreau. We would bicycle around, enjoy the city by day and candlelit bubble baths and booze by night, and then off again to the sights, sounds and people of Europe. During those months I met dozens of families, usually daughters first, and by the end of that year I had had the privilege of staying at least one night in over 60 different homes in nearly every country of Europe. Besides great food and hospitality there was time to consume useful expressions in languages like Swedish, German, French, Italian and later on Greek, mixed with English and bits of Haole Hawaiian. One of the greatest rewards reaped from all that unexpected European hospitality was the 53 Christmas cards I received after returning to California.

While in Copenhagen I made friends with a beautiful tall red headed prostitute who had more true life stories to share than Uncle Remus or Mark Twain. She wanted to write a book, a collection of confessions she was privy to while playing hostess but she was afraid it would require getting accepted into the witness protection program once published. We spent days roaming Copenhagen's back streets, or at Bente's house while she was at work. . . most of it innocent, just chatting. Amazing what a prostitute, hair solonist or cosmetologist can be told while working. . . . my stories pale by comparison.

My first introduction to the ways and beauty of Scandinavian women was not in Denmark but rather a tall statuesque blond walking alone along some shore in Honolulu. You wonder why I was so often on bikini patrol, and what a bikini. . . . a couple of strings wrapped around a statuesque serene tall blond, like the girl from Ipanema. Not so tan, but young and lovely, from a place called Denmark, that same place I was now living in. This beautiful Danish product was on her second free spirited tour around the world, modeling here and there to pay for her globe trotting until one sad day she was brutally murdered hitch hiking in Thailand. I talked about this lady one night with my new proprietor and lover, Bente, and asked if she had ever heard about a Danish model getting stabbed to death near Bangkok and in the morning she asked, "Did you mean Dorette Von Haeven?" Bente said everyone in Denmark knew about it. She even knew the girl's parents. I still had several photos of her from Hawaii, old Kodak shots from our days together including one Hawaiian luau. What about taking those pictures to Dorettes' parents? Not a good idea Bente said. Let it be. And that was that. What a sad waste of a beautiful lady and life. . . . It's easier for guys to roam around this planet alone than for women. . . especially good looking women like Dorette. . .

Her story was cut short. . . . never told. . . so true for so many,

Back to work, delivering those cars around Europe. Making money while sleeping in the back seats or in youth hostels, easy rider on four wheels. I received the gas money for each car delivered to and from Copenhagen or between cities in Europe. . . but that would not have covered my meager expenses. Extra coin was collected when a city stored more than one car waiting to be driven to another destination, or back to Copenhagen. If there were two or three cars in need of drivers I would go into the local youth hostel and yell out to all those backpackers that I was looking for drivers, a free car to some city in Europe, usually Copenhagen. It was an offer they couldn't refuse! One driver's license and passport was required, two contracts, one for the driver, one for me, keys, check out the car and off they go, happy to be back on the highways of Europe, for free. What those kids didn't realize was that gas or benzine was included, part of the deal. . . and it was that gas allowance that subsidized most of the 100,000 miles I traveled throughout every country of Europe save for Russia and Northern Ireland, two places I've still yet to visit. European countries are like states, sometimes smaller, but each offers a different culture, language, cuisine, customs, landscapes, traditions and of course ladies. Lots and lots of beautiful ladies most of which did not require as much chatting up as those littering the beaches of Hawaii. . . .

One of the highlights of traveling Europe that year was Prague. Paris was equally beautiful but Prague was different, especially back during the Cold War, hidden behind the Iron Curtain, darker, drearier, dirtier, and more intriguing. Eastern Europe at that time was like a time warp. People in Czechoslovakia were suffering, living for the moment, a censored existence, not realizing the material things they were missing. But deprivation is a mixed blessing. Eastern Europe did not realize fully the good and the bad of being deprived. Television channels were run by the State, Communist controlled, and reality was censored offering no variety and little or no hope. Limited travel and dreams. But plenty of good cheap beer, conversation and sex. Life was narrowly confined yet being broadly lived, an attitude lost on the West. Appreciation of the here and now existed in Prague and Eastern Europe while it was buried in the overabundance of the West. . . . . . When you can have anything and everything all the time it means little. As I write this the world is going through the Coronavirus Pandemic. . . . and it's the first time I have witnessed the Western World learning how to cope with less, suddenly being limited, humbled by fear and some deprivation, realizing how spoiled we were, how quickly life can change and become limited. . . Never to be deprived of wealth and material abundance is never to appreciate it. Of course the Czechs would happily have traded their restricted life behind the Iron Curtain for what the West was enjoying. But for 40 years they had no choice but to deal with their depression and make the most out of less. . . . . food, shelter, laughter, booze and sex. It was a great place to visit, which I did 22 times. For the Czech people I was a walking talking Time or Newsweek magazine and during those many visits Czechs wanted to hear everything. It was just different. Intriguing and romantic. After Czechoslovakia became the Czech Republic and Prague became more over run with tourists than Paris, I never returned.

The most special moment in all my travels took place one cold dark wet winter's night in an ally way in Prague, probably 1973. It happened on what is called Sylvester, named after the Pope Sylvester, a Roman Pope who's saint's day falls on December 31st, what is now know as New Year's Eve. It also happens to be the one day that Czech people in this land locked country enjoy a fish dinner, usually carp. After so many visits to Prague the idea of coming back as Santa Claus was added to my bucket list. As I had so little money my first year of travels in Europe, it was put off till the second winter. I was able to buy 100 Swiss chocolate bars, cartons of cigarettes, cigars, a bottle of Cognac, odd necklaces and then 10 large Swedish chocolate bars. There was nothing in the Kelty backpack but two Levi pants, treasured back then in all Eastern Europe, a couple of socks, underwear and all the Christmas presents. I barely got through the border crossing in East Germany, where they did a strip search and asked why all the chocolate bars? Fortunately even the hard ass East Germans had heard of Christmas. . . Weihnachten and they let me through.

Once in Prague I would ride the trolleys or trams with my cowboy hat and shoulder bag loaded with chocolate bars and when I saw a kid with his or her parent I would pull out a bar and say, "vesele Vanoce a stastny novy rok"... Merry Christmas and Happy New Year. The kids and parents would light up like Christmas trees and that Christmas Eve I was invited to at least three Christmas dinners. By the end of week on that Sylvester night I had only one big Swedish chocolate bar left, called Marabou. That bar was saved for my favorite girlfriend in Prague. But that night on my way back to my little suburb apt. I could see an old lady with two big shopping bags and a backpack looking through the trash cans. It was dark and rain was falling and it bothered me to see this on a night when most were celebrating Sylvester, New Year's Eve. After a cup of tea I walked a friend back to the tram stop and once again passed the alley with the old lady looking in the trash. On the way home I saw her for a third time and wondered what I could do to help? In the apt. I grabbed that last big Marabou Chocolate bar with 100 Swedish kroner and headed back out. She was still there about half way down this dark alley under the lone light bulb that hung from a wire swaying back and forth in the wind and rain. I was apprehensive knowing that few people in Czechoslovakia spoke English. As she searched through another trash can I tapped her on the shoulder. She turned with her bags and backpack and I held out my hand with the chocolate and money and said, "vesele Vanoce a stastny novy rok."She looked at the candy and money and then looked up at me and said in very plain English, "I can't take that, it's too much!" It stunned me to hear English coming from this old gray haired woman in an ally and I mumbled something like, "are you speaking English?" She said she was once a school teacher before the Russians took over and before she lost her husband. I asked why she was there and what she was looking for? She explained that it was just temporary, that she had lost her job and that whatever she needed was available in those trash cans, that it was OK for now and things would soon be better. She was not angry, not bitter, and not negative, in fact she used a word that I had never ever heard in all my travels, and she said it was her Karma. She accepted her plight. I handed her the chocolate and money saying this was her Christmas present and she needed to take it for my sake more than for hers. The gift of giving is always greater than the value of the gift. She looked at me with her two front teeth pointing south under a scarf and gray scraggly hair, rain dripping off her face and said something right out of a movie, "this is the best Christmas present ever."It was such a special moment. I then asked her if she wanted to come to my apt. for a bowl of warm soup or a warm shower and she looked into my eyes and told me, "I just want to remember the moment the way it is!"We gave each other a hug, both adding tears to the rain running down our cheeks, wished each other a Happy New Year and parted. When I got back to the apt. I was still shaking and crying and had to let it out by relating what just happened as best I could in a letter to my Grandmother.

It was by far my greatest Christmas memory. The gift of giving is so precious and rare and this one was clearly a reward for making the effort to be Santa Claus in Prague. . . . It was as close as I will probably ever come to meeting God.

After ending with the car delivery campaign I was anxious to get to some place with few tourists and lots of sun. I had about $150 and so after ending that winter as Santa Claus in Prague I decided to head for Greece via Eastern Europe. One of those lovely ladies I was dating in Prague just happened to work for the state travel agency and was able to hook me up with a $12 dollar student ticket that would carry me by rail from Prague, to Budapest, Hungary, to Bucharest, Romania, and end in Sophia, Bulgaria. It was early January, the dead of winter in a very cold part of the world and I had just given all my extra clothing away as Christmas presents, including two pair of Levis. I bought a cheap woman's leather coat in Prague, some driver's gloves with cut off fingers, second hand boots and off I went through the East in minus temps. First were the frozen dark streets of Budapest. I knew no one and needed a place to sleep so entered one of the finer hotels about midnight and told the nice young female receptionist that I was looking for a place to sleep. She said they had plenty of rooms and I responded by saying I didn't have plenty of money. She asked where I came from and I said the USA. She wondered why a Yank was traveling with no cash or charge cards and I told her. She took me to a storage room where all the dining room tables were kept and said I could sleep on any one of them but she would have to wake me early before getting off her night shift at 7am. That was how my first night went. The next day I was back on the rail headed for Romania. On the train I met a nice looking guy who was a student at the University of Bucharest. He spoke very little English but managed to invite me to stay in the student dorms on campus. We arrived late one freezing cold winter's eve and he left me standing outside the campus and went in to fetch a small army of fellow students who came out, surrounded me, and talked all of us past the guarded gates of the University. That night I was offered one of the 20 cotes lined opposite each other in a long cold dorm room. One cote, one locker per student and one strip of sausage or baloney hanging in the only window at the far end of the room. I was given a coat and an extra blanket. Sometime after midnight my friend woke me up and asked me to join about 30-40 students now surrounding one candle in the middle of the dorm room. It was time for the visitor to share with the few students who could understand English. What was going on in the Western World, a question and answer session that went on till dawn. For that I got treated to a nice slice of that hanging sausage. Besides words I was packing 12 tapes and an old battery operated Philips compact cassette recorder. Something like an EL-3302.

Among those 12 tapes were a couple from the Moody Blues, always my favorite band and one of their recordings was called Melancholy Man. The lyrics to that song must have hit a nerve to this one guy who played it over and over until the batteries went dead.

"I'm a melancholy man, that's what I am, all the world surrounds me, and my feet are on the ground.

I'm a very lonely man, doing what I can, all the world astounds me and I think I understand that we're going to keep growing, wait and see. . . . . . . "

Every morning I awoke in that military style student dorm room with an extra blanket over me and every day my new buddy gave me his jacket. It was a special three days that ended up at the same train station where it started. . . . a hug and a kiss good-bye. Romanian tradition. Last stop Sophia, Bulgaria. What a depressing place in 1971, especially in mid-winter. I stayed long enough to buy one hot dog and one $6 dollar train ticket to the Greek border on what turned out to be the milk run. That train stopped about every five miles all the way to the border. It loaded and unloaded anything and everything two legged and four legged. Goats, chickens, geese, dead or alive, pigs, dogs and humans, many of which were Mongolian. Short men with big ears. The dude sitting across from me was not Mongolian, he was huge, ugly and full of spit, most of which landed down around my feet. Nosiest, coldest and most uncomfortable train in all Europe yet I was sound asleep one hour out of Sophia. In the middle of the night the conductor woke me up, end of the line, the only person left on the train besides me and the engineer. We had to be near Greece so I ask the uniform. "Where is Greece, elinika, ellada, Hellenes, Zorba? ". . . a lot of arms flying around trying to dance like Zorba. Nothing. He points down the railroad tracks and walks one way, I walk the other. Looking back I notice that only one car was left on that relic of a train, the one I climbed out of. Twelve wooden cars departed Sophia, only one got to the finish line with its one passenger. Now to find Greece under a beautiful bright full moon. It was not just a street or town I was looking for, but an entire country, a fairly important one at that. I was walking the rails for about an hour when I came to a small border house where I woke up some guy in his pajamas. Passport control. . . . lol. So where is Greece I asked? He could care less but like the sleepy conductor he points down the same railroad tracks. A couple more hours walking the rails and I come to another hut, this one with a soldier. . . not in pajamas but in uniform with a rifle. Nervously I wake him up and ask the big question? Where is Greece? He points to the ground. Big smile all around. . . and waves me onward this time down a dirt road. Thirty minutes later I walk into my first Greek village. One house has a neon light that reads Politeia or Polis. Police. Inside the house is another uniform, this one sleeping on his desk. It was about 3 or 4 am and suddenly a guy with a backpack is standing in his station. He asks where I came from and I said Bulgaria. He wags his finger and says "ochi", no. He asks again after I show him my US passport. I repeat Bulgaria. He indicates in broken English it's not possible, no one ever comes from that direction. Bulgaria is part of Eastern Europe, one of the Soviet block countries. Hard to just walk out of, especially during the Cold War. . . and to this day it seems that a piece of that mysterious puzzle is missing. Still there I was, standing in Greece, after a miserable, I mean memorable, train ride through Czechoslovakia, Hungary, Romania, and Bulgaria ... all for a grand total of $18, topped off with a long walk under a beautiful bright full moon to my new home for the winter. The land of Zorba. The policeman told me to lay my sleeping bag on the station floor, and that was where I slept until the first bus arrived. This was typical Greek hospitality. The policeman said something to the bus driver and there was no charge for the Yank all the way to the city of Thessaloniki. Then another bus on to Athens for a quick look before boarding a ferryboat at the port city of Piraeus headed to the island of Crete. Again the cheapest ticket available, this one below deck with the farmers, animals and crops. ... no seating, no port holes. But before the boat departs I spot two beauties coming up the gangway dressed like they were headed for the Academy Awards in Hollywood, not some Greek island. The old gift of gab was there to welcome them aboard and before the mooring lines were tossed our trio was climbing staircases to the upper deck, opposite that lower deck, where their first class cabin bound for the historically famous island of Crete awaited. Better port holes than goat holes, better smell, better company. The overnight voyage in their suite was sweet. Once we arrived at the port of Heraklion on the north shore of Crete I quickly found a way to repay their hospitality. First to disembark, I spotted a flatbed wooden cart attached to a donkey which was attached to an old Greek, reins in hand. The uber rates were perfect and we took the cart over to the ferry to greet the two beauty queens coming down the gangway in heels and party dress. I escorted them to their open air coach, helped them board the boards and donkey driver took all of us to some fancy hotel on the other side of Heraklion. Another five star accommodation, five star delivery, five star boat ride and five star memory. Their hotel was four stars above my pay grade. One night in that place would have eaten my entire allowance for the winter. The money belt was hiding a little over $150.

A room more fitting my budget was in the village of Agios Nikolaos, a youth hostel filled with the usual hippies, back packers and ragged road runners, including one lady from Australia. The next day we teamed up, strolled to the East end of town, put our thumbs out on the only road encircling this oblong island, the largest in Greece. Soon a friendly Greek picks us up and somewhere past the town of Sitia drops us off out of sight of everything but olive trees. We asked what lay beyond the trees and he says water, in this case the Sea of Crete, a small part of the Mediterranean. We thanked him, grabbed our two packs and started walking north through the olive groves. After 30 minutes we were looking out over a rocky coastline and on the bluffs were planted three rock cottages spread out in the middle of absolutely nowhere. Perfect. We tap on doors and one of the three shelters is occupied by a friendly old Greek couple. Face and hand indications tell the couple we are looking for a place to stay and they offer us their dining room table, a wooden picnic bench. That night the two of us empty a pint of cherry flavored brandy, the worst tasting shit ever put in a bottle. What went down soon came back up, outside under that same fantastic full moon that helped guide me out of Bulgaria three nights earlier. The poor Aussie was upchucking half the night, a chorus of grunts blending with waves hitting the rocky shore below. . . . welcome to Crete.

The only reason I share this minor moment is the cute side bar that reminds us all how small this planet really is and how hard it is escape the endless parade of travelers constantly circling our tiny ball. After an egg, toast and cup of tea we wonder how to financially compensate our gracious hosts? No need to ask, the bill was waiting and before parting would we be so kind as to sign their guest book. . . . GUEST BOOK!! Yep, an old binder containing a few hundred names from all parts of the globe. What we thought was the great escape turned out to be just a very popular kitchen table that hundreds had slept on before us. We had joined the common vagabonds attempting to escape the common crowds. . . . so we thought. For a few moments we felt we were doing something really unique, sadly something hundreds of others had done before us. And this was in 1971. Imagine today. That old rocky house and kitchen table are probably a popular bed and breakfast. . . . book a year in advance!

I parted ways with the Australian lass and eventually end up hitching a ride to a tiny village in the Southwestern section of Crete called Chora Sfakion. No tourists in sight. All three small hotels are closed for the winter, leaving but one rocky two story house available to rent.

A run down structure with no indoor toilet, one light bulb, no stove, a decent kitchen table, an outdoor latrine or pit, all of it owned by an old widow in black I later named Krazy Kate. Six dollars a month. Yep $6. . . . utilities included. Nearly all women in Crete were old widows mostly a bproduct of WW II, so black was the dress code for elderly ladies. The Germans left hundreds of widows on Crete, along with one legged men, one arm, one eye, or combinations thereof. It also left a lot of Great War stories. Later I learned enough Greek to hear a few. Sfakion became home for the next four months. That outdoor l'eau was a tiny hut with a hole in the floor that welcomed gravity controlled turds to drop into "the valley of jolly brown giants,"a well fertilized ravine lined with neighboring huts and towering trees.

Four of the most memorable months of my life. No sex, just good food, good books, good exercise, good health, good habits, good solitude and good feelings. I soon transformed that rocky dwelling into a private restaurant for wayward souls, mostly fellow hobos that were hiking around the island. It became known as "Chad's Crazy Citchen" and the first 50 hobos were fed for free, a small attempt to compensate for being the perennial house guest all over Europe. Those first diners didn't bother to say thanks or help wash their own dishes so I ended up charging 25 cents a meal after that, including wine. One couple called me a bloody capitalist. About 100 more came by that winter and as far as I know nobody got sick or died, including the restaurant proprietor. I came to Crete with $150 and I left Greece 6 months later with $150, a full beard, a full belly and a full diary. It was the most I ever weighed in my life, 165 lbs. Eat, drink, read, write, exercise and sleep. . . in sweet solitude and near complete isolation.

A couple of memories from that time on Crete in Chora Sfakion are worth sharing. In order to resupply 'Chad's Crazy Citchen' it required a two day journey over the mountains to a main port along the northern coast, called Chania. I would catch a bus ride across the width of the island and stay overnight, then hit the morning street markets, fill the backpack with enough food to last two more weeks and start hitch hiking back. There was a small lighthouse on the end the rock jetty in Chania and that is where I would lay my sleeping bag, waving to the passing fishing boats into the sunset and again at sunrise. Markets opened early and everything was fresh and cheap. Veggies, lintels, pasta, honey, a little meat, whatever it took to make the four items on my non-existent restaurant menu. My favorite item in the market was a fantastic chocolate cookie. It would have been so easy to load the entire backpack with just those cookies. But there was room for only one bag every two weeks, about one cookie per day. That cookie and my Phillips cassette player helped teach me an interesting lesson on life. The batteries for the Philips were expensive and there were no electric outlets in my rocky castle. The lesson of living with less, enjoying it more. I was forced for the first time to discipline my needs, to regulate cravings. "He enjoys much who is thankful for little. "There became a chocolate cookie 'moment' as well as a 'music hour,' longed for each day, much anticipated and much enjoyed. If another bag of those cookies was but a few minutes away or if there was electricity available, those special moments would not have been special. Abundance cannot be appreciated or understood until its missing. . . gone. I have yet to live through a severe storm or fire or earthquake, so this bit of deprivation was as close as I had yet come to the concept of going without. For four months I was given an opportunity to make the most of what little was available. One chocolate cookie and a few minutes of music that suddenly became meaningful.

Abundance by deprivation.

Once every two weeks I would walk along the coast to the next tiny village called Lutro. A totally isolated hamlet of a dozen or so houses. One trip an old lady asked if I could help read a letter she had received from some relatives in the USA, her Uncle or Aunt or cousin. The letter was a Shakespearean tragedy, a sad soap opera. Her Uncle had nearly died in a fire accident that burned down the house. Someone else was sick in the hospital. Two pages of sadness that this old lady did not need or deserve. Why translate the truth? That old saying 'ignorance is bliss! 'I told her everyone was just ducky, all was good with her relatives over in the states. It put a smile on her face. Something we both needed. What the hell, she was already wearing black.

On every food run over the mountains to Chania I would stop in the same small village, the halfway house, and go into the same restaurant for an ouzo. The same old man was always there. He had lived in the states for years. Worked in the mines somewhere in Utah and only spoke Greek with his fellow workers. He had come back to this village on Crete for his remaining years. All that time in the USA, yet he spoke but a few dozen words of English. He matched my Greek perfectly. He would always call me over to his table with his ouzo. A few minutes of silence, then "hello American, how are you" then "how is the weather" followed by "what a beautiful day today", then "where was I going?" After some ouzo. In Greek 'ya mas' or 'eis igian.' A few minutes of silence would pass and then, hello American, how are you, it's a beautiful day today, where are you going? It became another favorite tradition, every two weeks. Whenever I came to that village kids would come up to me on the street and offer me boiled eggs or oranges. One day the kids ran right by me to some other guy further up the road who was also waiting to catch a ride to the north side of the island. I soon joined this blond curly haired guy and after a few minutes he says he has seen me somewhere before. It turned out we had both worked in the same place in Honolulu, at "Michel's" at the Colony Surf Hotel, a five star restaurant just below Diamond Head Crater. He managed to survive two nights. One of those many small world moments that we all have. He accepted an invitation to my humble $6 hotel / restaurant and ended up staying two weeks. In his backpack there was some corn meal from Switzerland so we started making cornmeal pancakes with honey and fresh yogurt. One morning we invited the neighbor to try a tiganita, Greek for pancake, and that became our morning tradition. Greeks feel obligated to return favors. It's a Greek custom to give back more than they take. He invited us both for a special dinner. That night there were two others who had come up for one of my 25 cent specials, and they were included on the neighbor's guest list. The wife was cooking inside, the husband pouring shots of ouzo for all of us outside. After six or seven ouzos the three Yanks were struggling to stay upright while our Greek host remained sober as a judge. I noticed something wet below his feet and after a couple more Greek/English exchanges, another 'ya mas' or eis igian was yelled out and I watched him toss his ouzo over his shoulder, adding to the damp spot on the rocks. He was getting his guests shitfaced or better prepared for the dinner special. Luckily.

Cuisine that night was to be the most favored parts of the lamb, the brains wrapped in the intestines with some stomach. Our female guest became an instant vegetarian and excused herself while the rest of us enjoyed this tasty chewy Greek specialty. No part of the lamb is ever wasted.

After nearly six months in Greece, mostly on Crete, I headed back north with the same amount of money that I arrived with, about $150. Even at a mere 25 cents per serving "Chad's Crazy Citchen" broke even. Once out of Greece it wouldn't last long. While delivering those cars around Europe that first year I met a nice jolly fun loving Swede who was selling water pumps in Eastern European countries. We met in in Czechoslovakia a couple of times and traveled across Poland and East Germany together. He always said if I was ever in need his door in Stockholm would always be open. So from Greece I hitched north across Europe to Sweden and arrived in the spring of 71'. By then I had about $50 left and knew only one profession, waiting tables. I went to the Sheraton Hotel in Central Stockholm and applied for a waiter's position. They said they needed help every summer but it would be necessary to speak some Swedish. My good friend John Borrfors had a lovely daughter, Monica Borrfors, who gave me a three day crash course in Swedish. Monica later became a famous jazz singer. She taught me a little more about Sweden than just the language. John had a relaxed trusting relationship with his daughter as did most Swedes with their kids back then. Around the world it was called "free love!" To a degree it was true back then. Sweden is the most agnostic country in the world and most Scandinavians to not carry God or parent complexes to bed with them as did most Americans. Americans were just as physical but needed time to internalize or rationalize everything first with God and family. With Swedes it was less complicated. If they liked you they went to bed with you. The physical and mental were not as separated back then.

Anyway after three days I went back to the Sheraton Hotel and got the waiter's position which was a tax free summer job good for 90 days. Sweden needed a lot of extra workers to fill positions their own people vacated during summer holidays. Swedes headed for country houses, yachts, and islands in the Stockholm Archipelago, second homes in Southern Europe or just typical holiday escapes.

Anyway I worked my 90 tax free days in Sweden and on that next to the last day was strolling through Stockholm trailing one of those lovely long legged Swedish blondes in a light colorful summer dress. As on bikini patrol in Waikiki I started chatting her up, sidewalk instead of shoreline. She was at least three inches taller than me. Five minutes into my song and dance she told me to relax, that she had had a dream the night before she was going to meet some Yank in Stockholm. We spent the rest of the day at one of those outdoor city pools and instead of packing up and pulling out of Sweden as my tax free summer work permit required I packed up and went with her by train to the town of Eskilstuna in the middle of Sweden to her small apt. with a big bathtub. She was a grammar school teacher and we spent the rest of the summer enjoying the fields and forests, the wine and the bathtub. When school started she invited me to come talk to her 6th graders about Hawaii. I explained that as a professional beach bum I had little to offer but she insisted so off I went that evening to the Eskilstuna library where some encyclopedias were sleeping and pulled out the one with H on it. For a few hours I read about the Sandwich Islands or Hawaii, an archipelago of eight major islands stretching 1,500 miles across the Pacific. The highest peaks, their names, the origins of the Polynesians, the language with only 12 letters in its alphabet. When it became a state. . . anything that might help me sound half way intelligent. It worked. Her classroom of curious students lit up like lights on a Christmas tree which in turn lit me up. . . . and planted a seed in that gray matter upstairs. That summer started with a Monica Borrfors and ended with a Monica Bjurefeldt. I took what was left of the Sheraton Hotel money and bought a one way ticket to New York City. There I found another one of those one way u-drive cars, this one headed south to Fort Lauderdale, Florida. I slept on beach chairs in Miami the first two nights while searching for a cheap room, preferably free. Before delivering the car in Miami I found an apartment complex owned by a trusting Christian couple that took me for my word. Sleep now pay later. . . get a job. They even tossed in an old bike and I peddled off in search of light labor. It did not take long. I found employment as a waiter at one restaurant, a dish washer at another and a bag boy at the local Publix Super Market. Three jobs. Though one restaurant soon fired me thinking I was stealing recipe (menu) ideas for the other restaurant where I was washing dishes. Then I got fired a couple of more times after telling restaurant mangers they were screwing their customers. Just couldn't keep my mouth shut when it came to my version of right and wrong. After running out of Turf and Surf or Top and Tail restaurants in Fort Lauderdale I bicycled up to Pompano to yet another Steak and Lobster place. The manager and I had a long chat during which he said that he had seen me somewhere before. Having been let go by places in Fort Lauderdale those were nervous words. It turned out I had served him the previous summer at the Sheraton Hotel clear over in Stockholm. Small world. I got the job and within two weeks had more than enough money to return to Hawaii. First to pay that lovely trusting couple for the room along with a bouquet of flowers. Two beautiful souls residing on planet earth.

The following is a page from an old diary. . . . written 11-25-71.

Fort Lauderdale, Florida

My apologies for a few repeats.

"Came back from Europe on Air Icelandic for $150 airfare that included three meals and chasers. Hit the dis-United States with $40 left in the pocket and took the Johnathan Winters bus to the first subway station closest to Kennedy Airport. Mike, met on the flight, and I were going to make the best of a long night on the streets of the Big Apple but were saved by a young lady who took us home to meet her parents right off the streets of mean old NYC. Shocking to find such spontaneous hospitality on the streets of the Big Apple. What a delightful way to be welcomed back to the USA. I actually found the same in Paris, another city with a bad rap. Next day we found a one way u-drive car needed in Miami and we headed south for the sunshine state, reaching those hotel lined sandy shores within 36 hours of landing in New York. From Europe to the deep South through beautiful

Virginia, North and South Carolina. We even visited a few Civil War Battle Fields before Mike jumped out in Tallahassee. I got to Fort Lauderdale two days before the car was due for delivery. Time enough to scout around, try to locate a job and place to stay. Two nights on beach chairs in front of a deluxe Miami Beach hotel and I was down to only $7. 00. After 10 days I was back up to $200 having found employment with two different restaurants and as a bag boy at Publix Market. The area was loaded with big cars, big homes, big yachts, big hotels and big bank accounts. It was hard to find a native Floridian. One of the nicer looking transplants in Fort Lauderdale was Linda. I ported her grocery bags out to another Lincoln Continental while yapping at her about the obliterated skylines, polluted canals and indifferent people. Instead of ignoring me like everyone else, she asked if I would like to continue the conversation later. We met after work and became great friends. Our common interests were the Moody Blues, environmental issues, physical needs and showers. The best part Linda turned out to be her X-husband. Jealousy was not an issue with Linda and her X, a unique middle aged big harry man who designed luxury yachts. He was loaded with money like most in those parts, including his own airplane, and he asked if I would to be his co-pilot to Exuma in the Bahamas OK. His destination was Little Exuma. After a scenic flight over the islands we landed, walked a beautiful beach dotted with lovely conch shells, then headed off to the island's finest restaurant. We decided to add a little spice to our evening meal. He was this big burly character with bushy wild hair, at least 6'3". Sasquatch reincarnated. We decided he would be allowed to say just one word. . . all night long. . . some word that made absolutely no sense. Something Germanic. We chose the word Grulich or Groolich. No meaning. Perfect. The waiter arrived to take the drink order. He asks Sasquatch and gets a nice big "Grulich". . . the waiter asks again and gets another Grulich. He looks at me. . . I shrug. Time to devise a new language to fit the occasion. I speak Swedish, badly, so with a slight twist in pronunciation it became Spitsbergenish. . . from the island of Spitsbergen off Northern Norway. Time to ask Sasquatch in Spitsbergenish what he wants to drink and he replies Grulich. I tell the waiter Rob Roy up. The waiter, waitress and bus boy each get 40 shades of Grulich. . . and we all get to hear my version of Spitsbergenish, which brings smiles and laughter all around, especially from Sasquatch. A tossed salad with roquefort dressing, fillete of fish with fresh vegetables and so on and on for two hours. Grulich, from soft and sweet and complimentary, to loud and grumpy, all of it funny and funnier. A couple of other tables start to tune in and ask where the big dude is from? I say Spitsbergen off Northern Norway in the Svalvard Archipelago in the Arctic Ocean. WHERE? There we were on Little Exuma in the Bahamas, just island hoping. We grinned through dinner drinks, desert and finally music. One of the ladies asked if Sasquatch would like to dance and he obliged. That was classic. His dancing skills equaled his communication skills.

Ode de joy. Beethoven and this guy looked a lot alike, different hair color. .

Back to Fort Lauderdale and Linda who was slightly pissed that her X had borrowed me for the week-end. No more happy showers, no more ode du joy with Linda so I located another one way u-drive car and departed Florida, heading West with my favorite three Moody Blues tapes.

I need to hurry up and finish this written journey. . . . as I sit here now the Coronavirus has changed the world as we know it in only three months . It's been a humbling and frightening experience for millions, actually billions, and a lethal< for thousands. As I write this there is no vaccine in sight. Our trio, my daughter, I and the rental lady have survived the first waves of the virus and are wondering what the following waves will be like across the USA and around the globe? I am also down to just one dog out of the four I had when starting this Nobel Prize for Literature.

If I don't reach the finish line soon I may have the change the name of my memoirs to "sleeping with the cat". .... A stray Bengal my daughter brought home a couple months ago. >

Time to steal another page from that old diary.

A recap of the previous 18 months. . . full circle.

San Juan Capistrano, Ca. 12-20-71

"The long lap has ended and now back to the future. Times change and they do their best to rearrange, nothing new, just the same old Dad doing the same old things. After 18 months around the world I was given 30 minutes to share a lifetime of adventures. . . then it was back to their world, the one I forgot existed. You can go out and experience a hundred lives on the road, but your greatest joys and sorrows will be shared alone. You soon will have to blend back into everyone else's reality, in this case home and family. You may want to hold onto those fresh memories as long as possible, but good luck. Even your greatest yesterday's soon take up residence on the back roads of your mind. They die quickly unless recorded, soon just part of the foggy forgotten past. . . . . and there they will perish for good unless you too decide to write about them. Hopefully you also kept a few diaries.

After a few months in So Cal I flew back over to Hawaii and settled in for two more years, once again waiting tables and popping corks while trying to get laid as often as everyone else visiting or living in Hawaii. . . it was now the 70's but not much had changed. Two years, that ain't long Hawaii. Times change and they do their best to rearrange. Just a little less of what was good before.

Don't look back you only see what they locked away.

Focus in and don't let them take away what's here today. . .

Couldn't get much better. Between dining, dashing and dipping, I put some slide presentations together that showed how much the islands had been changed, or destroyed, by tourism and economic development. Back then ecology was still a fresh topic, there was a huge interest in conservation, and Hawaii was a perfect example of how fast things can be lost or changed, landscapes and attitudes alike. My term for it was 'Human Ecology". How man was becoming a product of his own products, how thoughts, needs and behavior were all by-products of our immediate environments. People perform and behave in accordance with their surroundings. No choice. Dreams, books, movies and conversations can transport you to new places, but reality is pretty much what you see around you. As man changes the world he changes himself, maybe not intentionally. I put together several slide presentations that would visually prove how much Hawaii had been changed (destroyed} in thirty years. Attaching mental and emotional changes to the environmental ones was going to be the challenge. But these slide presentations became my ticket into the classrooms of Sweden, and a future. A couple of surfing films, a coconut, lava, one authentic grass skirt from Samoa, necklaces, kikepa, or tapa cloth, sarongs, twine woven from coconut husk, a head full of idealistic thoughts... and I was ready to go off and save the planet... . Hawaiian style.

After getting settled into Stockholm at the University dorms I found the head of the Stockholm school board and laid out my collection of Polynesian goods and thoughts. They loved the content, ideas and enthusiasm and said they would find some classrooms to help get me started in Stockholm but I said I preferred to go north to Lapland, to see how the isolated Sami or Lap cultures compared to the once isolated Hawaiian or Polynesian cultures. They gave me the name of some director living above the Arctic Circle and I jumped a train and headed for the small town of Boden. That director was leaving for a village even further north, above the Arctic Circle, called Jokkkmokk. And that is where my teaching career started, living in small folk schools in communities above the Arctic Circle exchanging programs on Hawaii for room and board. My very first presentation was to a class of 8-12 year old Lapp or Sami kids. Their English was the same as my Swedish, but they enjoyed the grass skirt, surfing film and a displaced hapa haole or white foreigner from the opposite side of the planet. Hawaii was 12 times zones away. Humble beginnings. I was not a teacher, no degrees, no experience in front of groups, audiences, students or anything bigger than a track squad or football team. Time was needed to polish up the presentations and what better place than Lapland. A cute side note came from Jokkmokk. The town is an isolated mostly Sami village of less than 2000, living in the dark all winter save for the few street lights and the moon. They had a museum with some of the oldest skis on the planet and very few guest speakers, especially from Hawaii. So after giving talks in the grammar schools some teachers decided to invite the whole community to the museum for a special presentation. There was the museum with at least 100 chairs all lined up, lights on, nice and toasty inside and about 30 below outside, winds tossing the snow sideways past the street lamps in a blizzard and yet somehow two people managed to defy the elements and show up. . . front row seats. The girl was the one I had placed the grass skirt on at a school the day before, and her mother. A special night. Just the three of us, plus the museum curator.

A couple other slices of serendipity need mentioning. These grammar schools wanted to pay me even while I insisted that I was not there to exchange my dreams for sliver and gold. But they insisted and so I agreed to the minimum per classroom. The last school was in the biggest town above the Arctic called Kiruna and there I was sent to apply for a work permit. The official I met with in town asked what I was talking about in the schools. I offered something about how man was changing so many parts of the earth and in turn was being changed himself. . . what I called human ecology. He said it sounded like I might be some kind of environmental researcher. . . . "Miljöforskare" in Swedish.

Perfect, and that is what I became on all future work permits for the next 14 years in Sweden. An invited non-tax paying environmental researcher. That work permit allowed me to return to Sweden every year and present programs in the high schools or as they are called in Sweden gymnasiums. I went on to visit over 100 different gymnasiums and spoke personally to over 60,000 students in towns and cities from the top of Sweden, Lapland, to the bottom, Skona, the cities of Lund and Malmo. It was the most satisfying rewarding period of my life, the dream of motivating others with words and pictures. I did not remain the hula hula director for long, but those items and photos from Hawaii opened the door and it was Monica from Eskilstuna that gave me the key when she invited me to her grammar school classroom. . . we both had our dreams come true. For her a Yank for a few summer days. For me teaching and then traveling for the next 45 years.

The other thing that happened in Kiruna or Lapland besides the work permit was a camera, my first with a detachable lens. Some traveler from Czechoslovakia was selling an old Nikon F with a 35mm lens and it was love at first sight, a love that transformed me into a freelance photographer. Those Nikon kids kept me company all over the planet, a partnership that allowed me to avoid time clocks and bosses. It also allowed me to find some of those glossy pages from all the National Geographic Magazines Grandpa kept.

Back in the 70's there were probably only a couple hundred full time highway hobos shooting what was called "stock photography." Photo agencies were all over the world, Mom and Pop image libraries that desperately needed new material and were willing to pay 50% of sales to their contributors. It made travel photography cost effective, just take the Nikon kids on the road with a tripod and a couple of lenses and collect royalties the rest of your life. Too good to believe. At its peak my images were selling for over a million dollars a year, four years in a row, well over $40,000 per month and in that period I never sold a single photo myself, just the artist, not the salesman. No work for hire, no weddings, no bar mitzvahs, no families on the beach, no dogs, no restraints. Take as many photos as possible and survive. Travel, see the world, meet people, buy food, film and equipment, get good processing, label all the 35mm slides, send them out, clean the camera and get ready to go again. It was nice while it lasted. Marriage was the beginning of the end. So was digital photography. For me it went from a million dollars a year to nearly nothing. What happened? The digital age, Photoshop, computer enhanced images, cellphone cameras, everyone could do what the professionals once did. Mom and Pop photo agencies got devoured by the big boys like Getty and Corbis. Deep pockets and bad management. Humans and cameras became expendable as did millions of good images. From a 50% split with photographers to 40% to 30% to 20% to 10%. . . . to pennies per sale. Copyright laws no longer protected images, or photographers. More images were being stolen off the internet than were being paid for. What Amazon did to brick and mortar, Getty and others did to small stock agencies and photographers. It was no longer cost effective to be a stock photographer. . . . but hey, I got on board early when there were plenty of seats on the gravy train, rides were cheap, the world safer, less crowded and photographs were paid for. Our images were all real, done in the camera. Now, like so many other art forms, purity and reality became rare, purity a rare species, control gone and so was the money.

Why complain? I arrived to Sweden with $50 and left a millionaire with seven books published and found a profession I loved, something I would happily have done for free. Loving to go to work is a rare privilege.

"You can only become truly accomplished at something you love."

"Never continue in a job you don't enjoy. If you're happy in what you're doing, you'll like yourself, you'll have inner peace. And if you have that, along with physical health, you will have more success than you possibly could have imagined". . . . Johnny Carson.

Once again it all started on a chance meeting with a beautiful blond in Stockholm in the summer of 71'.

There are a few other special experiences that should be tossed into this salad before leaving the kitchen.... One was put into a short travel story called "A Bicycle Journey Across the USA".

Something I did with a Swedish boy I had met while hiking in the Arctic Wilderness a couple you years earlier. His name was Jan Danielsson and we met while trying to cross a stream that was acting up a bit during another rainy day in Lapland. We helped each other navigate the stream with our backpacks on our heads and continued our teamwork for two more summers in the North of Norway and Sweden. He became my only hiking buddy and was very much a part of my first photography book, "Snail's Trail". After that second summer he suggested we try something a different, a new mode of adventure travel, a bicycle trip. This he was good at but something I had not done since my grammar school paper route. Being a long distance runner and now hiker it sounded easy and so we agreed to bicycle together the next summer across the states. We met up in Philadelphia, he flew over with his bike from Sweden and I took the Greyhound from California with my Centurion in a box. We put our bikes together in friends garage in that city of 'Brotherly Love' and off we went, from the East Coast back to where I started on the West Coast. We traveled about 4,000 miles, met some of the finest people on earth, jumped a freight train with our bikes in Minot, North Dakota, rode in an empty box car through the Badlands of Montana then into Glacier National Park and jumped off at Whitefish. We tried to max our visit to Glacier National Park by going East over Logan Pass across the Continental Divide then West through Idaho along the Lachsa River to the Columbia River where it merged with the Snake and Yakima Rivers at Pasco, Washington. There we were allowed to jump a tugboat with our bikes for passage down the Columbia River through the five big locks to Portland, Oregon. We remounted the bikes and finished off the journey riding South along the Pacific Ocean into California. At the end of that 6 week adventure, one of my favorites, I wrote the following.

"Along with every effort we make. . . be it with animals, handicapped children, the young or old, with music, books or art, with sports, hobbies, camping, boating, bicycling, with any adventure, we again in experience, knowledge and confidence all of which builds character, usually a better one. These deposits we make into our personal banks are what we draw from the rest of our lives. "The brain is our bank" and everyone needs to make as many deposits as possible, as early as possible. Call it the compounded interest factor.

We have just printed some vivid images on our minds, moments from 4,000 miles of peddling bikes will remain forever, to draw from when the time or conversation is right. The photos will help and the diary will store things the mind cannot. It will always remain a part of our personal bank account, one that later can provide a different kind of social security.

Money vs. Memories. Memories do not pay the bills but money without such memories can be empty and meaningless. Owning things vs. doing things?

We go out on these adventures ultimately by ourselves and for ourselves, but it is the sharing with others that stimulates and rewards our efforts. The family in Stroudsburg, Pa., the little leaguers, the grocer in Wycox, the bicycle shop in London, Ontario, the Babcocks, the farm in Michigan, the restaurant in Brown City, the station master in Minot, the endless number of individuals that offered food, a meal, a shower, conversation and encouragement, or a place to sleep. People make the difference and provide reason for going places. When you travel, wherever you go, it is usually the people you remember, not the place. Within a few days after our return I mailed out over 20 thank-you cards to some of the many who shared their time and hospitality with our passing duo. Before we began this journey I had built up quite a negative image of the USA, having lived in Europe the previous 6 years, weary of the long lethal involvement in Vietnam, the cold war in Russia, the mess in Iran and the Middle East, the Watergate cover-up, Nixon, and just our general posture toward other countries. "Love it or leave it" was a popular saying. . . . . so I left it! When I came back and bicycled across it I found the USA filled from coast to coast with warm, friendly, generous individuals, as hospitable and caring as anywhere on earth. Jan was in shock the whole trip. The decency offered came from complete strangers, not just fellow travelers as you might expect in campgrounds, motels and RV parks. The people we met rejuvenated my outlook toward my own country, something much needed and much appreciated.

And the fulfillment of a journey is found along the way, not at the end, the effort being the biggest part of the reward. Goals are important, all kinds. Riding a bike across the states was a goal, a bit different from hiking an Arctic trail. Now it's over and yesterday's accomplishments never satisfy today's longings. Ask any writer who completes a book, a painter who completes a painting, a traveler who completes a trip. The sense of satisfaction does not last. It is the next book, the next painting, the next adventure that is important. Yearnings are healthy. As long as your heart is receiving messages that are filled with joy, excitement and curiosity, you are healthy and alive. When that thinking becomes burdened with pessimism and doubt, and prevents you from taking risks your soul starts aging along with your body.

May there always be one or two goals growing inside. . . and as for why bother writing diaries. . . or this memoir called "Sleeping With The Dogs? "

Perhaps my daughter will someday discover that her Dad did other things before the advent of getting to school on time, finishing homework, cleaning up, arguing, paying bills, taking care of four legged critters, burying small ones in the back yard under a rose plant, carrying the bigger ones to a vet to be put down, crying all the way home. . . . .

This is written with the hope she might someday record her own experiences and adventures in her computer to be shared with my Grandchildren... who I hope to live long enough to meet. As of this ending there is only one dog left, Muggsie, along with the stray Bengal cat that my daughter found, Simba.

One turtle, Taco, and one bearded dragon, Lucky. All the two legged critters here outlived the four legged ones. No coronavirus. Life's good.

To summarize: The best parts of the past as far as travel and adventure goes were the many summers hiking in the Arctic Wilderness in the north of Sweden and Norway known as Lapland. Next would be the bicycle journey across the USA with Jan. Third would be the three whitewater trips down the Colorado River through the Grand Canyon in the dories, each journey at least 14 days. Fourth was a horse and cart holiday around the Dingle Peninsula in County Kerry, Ireland with my Irish girlfriend Annie Donahoe, (the same Annie that nearly drowned under one of those Grand Canyon Dories when it flipped in a whirlpool on the Colorado River,) her Mother Bridie, and our unpredictable monstrous four legged motor Molly, the Draught Horse that led the way.

Traveling around the world for over 40 years added to the smorgasbord that filled out a life leading up to that cul de sac in Laguna Niguel. . . .

Now I wait and watch while the dogs, dog, grows older, the daughter grows older and the insurance rates and taxes grow higher.

So it goes.

Before this keyboard produces writers cramps one more time I need to give a shout out to a couple of people that helped guide my life and supplied the courage and motivation and love to go out and do these things. One was my handicapped sister, Robyn. She started her life with cerebral palsy (a condition marked by impaired muscle coordination (spastic paralysis) and/or other disabilities, typically caused by damage to the brain before or at birth.)

From birth she was never able to talk or hear but she could communicate in her own way, especially with family. She was a motivating force in all our lives. I have so often listened to others, usually great athletes being interviewed on TV who also grew up with a special needs person, usually a sibling, at how their lives were effected for the better, how by comparison they learned to more fully appreciate things that so many take for granted. People who grow with handicapped siblings or friends are fortunate. They are usually inspired to try harder, appreciate good health, enjoy the little things and take more chances. My sister died from pneumonia at age 44. She loved to compete in the handicapped Olympics and without knowing it she helped show others how to appreciate life, to live it to its fullest potential. I found an old letter I wrote to her after she passed away.

> Dear Robyn,
>
> For all the years you were here as my sister I never had the chance to communicate to you with words. I am going to take a little chance here and assume that there is such a thing as reincarnation and that you have a spirit that still lives, that your soul, or spirit, or whatever we try to name it, has now taken up residence in a healthy body. . . . at last. One that can hear and talk, run and walk normally. By now you may well want to forget that previous body you

were forced to drag around for over 40 years, but hopefully you still remember some of us who loved you back then.

You have no idea of how many extra laps of the track I ran thinking of you, especially those tougher laps, the last one in the mile race, the one where weaker spirits slow down. How often I carried a thought of you to some higher level in the mountains when the climbing got harder. I talked of you hundreds of times in the classrooms to thousands of students trying to give them a better sense of appreciation for the little things; the privilege of just being able to hear, to talk or walk, to taste, touch, see and above all feel, joys we could all easily take for granted were it not for people like you who were here to remind us that nothing is guaranteed, take nothing for granted.

You finally did give up after 44 years. You had lived long enough in that broken wreck of a body, a Porsche spirit in a VW body.... you spent enough time in physical purgatory. It was time to live in a whole anatomy, to go to health clubs instead of chiropractors, jump over things instead of falling over them, to start to enjoy what you spent so many years here trying to teach others to enjoy. Maybe you can get back here to give some of us more inspiration before our time comes to check out... as if you hadn't given enough already."

And then the most influential people in my life, my Grandparents, mostly my Grandmother, Audria Stimpson. They were there from the start in Manhattan Beach, California, owners of the courtyard apartments where my Mother lived and where my older brother and I were born and raised. I spent my first 11 years living next door to them, collecting their love and enjoying those summers of camping in Northern California which I have already talked about. Grams had something special called Agape love, the highest form of love and charity, unconditional. I have never found it in any other soul since, but you sometimes read and hear about others who also offered such selfless love.

I believe she might have developed such an attitude when she came so close to dying from smallpox in her early 20's. This infectious disease was caused by the variola virus, a lot worse that today's coronavirus. It was a disfiguring and usually deadly disease and when Grandma became infected they quarantined her where Dodger Stadium now sits at Chevez Ravine in one of the many quonset huts used to isolate severe smallpox patients. Audria had one of the worst cases ever to survive and it was in part due to her nurse, some Australian woman who took eggs from a nearby chicken farm and the poured the raw eggs loaded with zinc, iron and copper down Grandma's throat as she lay burning up. Grams was badly disfigured having lost her fingernails, toenails and hair, so much so she was too embarrassed to stay among friends in Southern California so she moved to some relative's ranch in Canada for three years while her skin regenerated. Granddad or Lucious Charles Stimpson, who loved her long before she had small pox was still waiting and they married, sharing the next 65 years together. What must have influenced Grandma's love of life and charitable character was her long dance with death. People infected with the coronavirus must be dealing with similar fears and thoughts now.

After Manhattan Beach Grandma ended up in Leisure World in Seal Beach where she became known as the "Soup Lady", making soup for those that were sick or suffering in the neighborhood. She never expected anything in return, not even a thank you. Her rose garden was the Versailles of Leisure World. She always treated plants and animals as she would her fellow man.

Agape love.

So what about all these years since divorce and starting to write these memoirs? I certainly failed at becoming the 'dog whisperer'. Four dogs when I started this project, one left. One teenage daughter when I started, fortunately one left, now 22 and sleeping, eating and making a living with her computer and musical talents. Still shooting my age in golf, now and then. The big change for this old golf fart was the art of getting scammed. Yes, at every age the internet became the new means of communicating with the rest of the world and if you joined one of those dozens of dating sites you know what cyberspace relationships are all about... giving money away! ! Yes, receiving an endless supply of fabulous photos and messages from ladies that were most likely sent by guys. Cyberspace became the new Wild West for scammers. Lawless with very few sheriffs around to help guard against fraud and extortion. It was and is fertile ground for people just like me, single, old, horny and with nowhere to go to meet others save for Trader Joe's or the local coffee shops which became a collection of people looking like bank robbers, all wearing masks. Yep, the on-line dating sites became the new fishing grounds for people of all ages and they were teaming with sharks. Syndicated crime took over the fishing grounds just like the Asians did the high seas. I doubt there is a person alive today with a computer that has not lost money to dating site scams, oftentimes big money. My fish line went into a dating site called POF.

"Plenty of Fish" offered some of the most contaminated cyberspace waters on the internet. The need to chase women was part of my psychic since those days on bikini patrol in Waikiki and after divorce those habits went unchecked even while the testosterone tank was nearly empty. My mind continued trying to write checks that the body could never cash. Getting involved time and again with younger ladies that sent gorgeous photos along with a myriad of plausible stories. They turned me into one of those human ATM machines. The Red Cross for anyone with big boobs. The naive old golf fart. No matter how many friends, including my daughter, tried to tell me that the photos did not belong to the person sending the messages, I would not listen. Going long distant fishing in such places and Ghana and Nigeria or other parts of the USA was just too much fun, too tempting. It all felt good... for about the first $30,000. Then it felt stupid. After five years of playing the village idiot and being duped at least 50 times, it was not quite as entertaining or rewarding. Cyberspace relationships will drain you emotionally, mentally and especially financially. Today it's a billion dollar business. For some, like me, it went from getting playfully scammed to attempted extortion. It went from fun to frightening and eventually I reported the accumulated threats to the police fraud department, changed my phone number, got out of Google Hangouts, deleted some names and started blocking emails. For the first time ever I was locking my doors at night. Cyberspace relationships are not healthy for the old and naive. What's next? Who knows? The coronavirus changed life as we knew it. The world was sent into quarantine. An invisible meteorite struck our little planet with a vengeance.

We all are now wondering what the 'new normal' will be?

Even sleeping with that last dog, Muggsie, has changed. She now sleeps under the bed. . . the cat sleeps on top.

And now she is gone. . . . Yep, Muggsie, the last dog ran out of gas.

I know the feeling.

"Send in the dogs.
Where are the dogs?
There ought to be dogs.
Well maybe next year."

LIST OF PHOTOGRAPHS - LOCATIONS